PrayerFoundation Evangelical Lay Monks ™

Prayer as a Celtic Lay Monk
Learning from Celtic Christian Prayer

by S.G. Preston

*"Let my prayer arise
before You as incense,
and the let the
lifting up of my hands,
be as the evening offering."*

-Psalm 141:2

———

*"I arise today,
through a mighty strength,
the invocation of the Trinity;
through belief in the Threeness,
through confession of the Oneness
of the Creator of Creation."*

-St. Patrick's Breastplate Prayer

2nd Edition

PrayerFoundation Press ™
Vancouver, WA 98687 U.S.A.

There are a few references to fasting in this book. Some people should never fast: pregnant women, the sick, those with diabetes and certain other medical conditions. Before fasting, check with your Physician first, to learn if this is something you can safely do.

ISBN-13: 978-09995307-4-0

Preston, S.G., 1951-

PrayerFoundation Evangelical Lay Monks ™
Prayer as a Celtic Lay Monk
Learning from Celtic Christian Prayer

1. Prayer. 2. Celtic Christianity. 3. New Monasticism.
4. Christian History. 5. Evangelicals. 6. Threefold Daily Prayers.

Print Edition and eBook Edition
created for publication by:
PrayerFoundation Press ™

Published by:
PrayerFoundation Press ™
Vancouver, WA 98687
Email: monks@prayerfoundation.org

Books by S.G. Preston:

PrayerFoundation Evangelical Lay Monks ™
Series:

Prayer as a Total Lifestyle:
Learning from the Greatest Lives of Prayer

Prayer as a Celtic Lay Monk:
Learning from Celtic Christian Prayer

Answers to Prayer:
A Global 24-Hr. Prayerchain Since 2000

————

These books have been written to inspire and motivate you to draw
nearer to God in prayer.

Interspersed with a generous selection
of the best quotations from some of

The Greatest Lives of Prayer
the books can also be used as a Daily Devotional.

Their extensive Indexes (in the Print Versions) make them useful as
Reference Works.

They have been written in a clear, concise, easily understood style to
make them suitable as a thoughtful *"prayer encouragement"* gift
for friends, relatives, and young people.

Dedicated to:

My wonderful, loving Christian mother…
Carol Ann Preston

———

Our Mission:

*"To Promote Prayer Among All Christians
and Proclaim Christ to the World."*

Scripture Basis:

*"But we will devote ourselves continually to prayer,
and to the ministry of the word."*

-Acts 6:4

Learning from Celtic Christian Prayer

Aidan's Prayer

*"Leave me alone with God
as much as may be.*

*As the tide draws the waters
close in upon the shore,
make me an island, set apart,
alone with You, God, holy to You.*

*Then, with the turning of the tide,
prepare me to carry Your presence
to the busy world beyond,
the world that rushes in on me,*

*until the waters return
and enfold me back to You."*

-St. Aidan of Lindisfarne
(c. 600-651 A.D.)
Irish Monk who converted
Northern England to Christ

Contents:

4. *One Daily Hour of Prayer*

5. *Abiding in Christ*

6. *How to Pray the Psalms*

A Very Brief Introduction

"...the simplicity that is in Christ..."

-2 Corinthians 11:3

Prayer as a Celtic Lay Monk

So just what is *"Prayer as a Celtic Lay Monk"*? What exactly do we mean when we say that it is how we live our life in Christ? This book, and our entire Ministry, is easily summarized:

Knowing Christ is the Essence of Christianity.
Prayer is the Essence of the Christian Life.

God's Will for Our Lives

"Rejoice always. Pray without ceasing. In everything give thanks. For this is the will of God in Christ Jesus concerning you."

–1 Thessalonians 5:16-18

Christ's Great Commission

"And He said to them, 'Go into all the world and proclaim the Good News to everyone."

-Mark 16:15

Be Holy, for I am Holy

"But as He who has called you is holy, so be holy in everything you do. Because it is written, be holy, for I am holy."

-1 Peter 1:15-16

The Nicene Creed

"We have the universal faith in the Creed, known to the faithful and committed to memory, contained in a form of expression as concise as has been rendered admissible by the circumstances."

-St. Augustine of Hippo (354-430 A.D.)

Our Statement of Faith

Our Statement of Faith can be seen in Section 9.3. We describe our *PrayerFoundation*™ Ministry as a *"Mere Christianity"* Ministry, summed up in this quote by C.S. Lewis:

> *"Ever since I became a Christian I have thought that the best, perhaps the only, service I could do for my unbelieving neighbors was to explain and defend the belief that has been common to nearly all Christians at all times."*

But you say, all of that is just *basic, essential Christianity!* Yes, that is what Celtic Christianity and Celtic Lay Monasticism is to us.

The Missionary Bishop, St. Patrick, converted Ireland to Christ, using a monastic Celtic Christian framework. The Celtic Christians of Ireland then sent thousands of *Missionary Monks* (the *"green martyrs"* who left their homeland to proclaim the Gospel) throughout Europe. They converted pagan Northern Europe to Christ for the first time, and re-converted a Southern Europe reverted to pagan barbarism.

We have adopted this same monastic Celtic Christian framework, but put it through the lens of the Protestant Reformation and Evangelicalism.

Our Mission:

> *"To Promote Prayer Among All Christians and Proclaim Christ to the World."*

> *"But we will devote ourselves continually to prayer, and to the ministry of the word."*

-Acts 6:4

That is what this book is all about! May God bless you through it!

Yours in Christ,

S.G. Preston
(Lay Monk Preston)
Vancouver, Washington
St. Patrick's Day, 2020

26

Irish Celtic Christian Monk Poems

"Is acher ingáith innocht... Fufuasna faircggae findfolt.
Ni ágor réimm mora minn dondláechraid
lain oua lothlind."

Vikings

"Bitter is the wind tonight... It tosses the ocean's white hair.
Tonight I fear not the fierce warriors of Norway
coursing on the Irish Sea."

-Old Gaelic Monk's Poem (c. 850 A.D.)

———

"Messe ocus Pangur Bán, cechtar nathar fria saindán:
bith a menma-sam fri seilegg, mu menma céin im saincheirdd..."

-Old Gaelic Monk's Poem (c. 850 A.D.)

Pangur Bán

"I and Pangur Bán my cat, it's a like task we are at:
hunting prey is his delight, hunting words I sit all night.

Better far than praise of men, is to sit with book and pen.
Pangur bears me no ill will; he too plies his simple skill.

It's a merry task to see...at our tasks how glad are we;
when at home we sit and find...entertainment to our mind.

Oftentimes his prey will stray...in the hero Pangur's way;
oftentimes my keen thought set...takes a meaning in its net.

Against the wall he sets his eye, full and fierce and sharp and sly;
against the wall of knowledge I, all my little wisdom try.

When his prey darts from its den, O how glad is Pangur then!
O what gladness do I prove, when I solve the doubts I love!

So in peace our task we ply; Pangur Bán my cat, and I.
In our arts we find our bliss; I have mine, and he has his.

Practice every day has made...Pangur perfect in his trade;
I get wisdom day and night...turning darkness into light."

Answers to Prayer
PrayerFoundation ™ 24-Hr. Prayerchain

Mar. 29, 2004 - Answer To Prayer:

We here at the *PrayerFoundation* ™ were watching the News today, and heard them announce that Mel Gibson's film, *The Passion of the Christ,* which had been banned from being shown in France, would now be allowed to be seen there.

We had reported this ban on our website a month ago, but could find no confirmation of the banning from any other source.

Our own information came to us from Jim Caviezal, the actor who plays Christ in the film, through a friend of his. We could find no other mention of it, either by News sources, or even on Internet postings.

Our thanks to those of you who prayed with us for the French ban to be lifted.

-PrayerFoundation Lay Monks ™
Knights of Prayer Lay Monastic Order ™
Vancouver, Washington

(From the book: *Answers to Prayer* by S.G. Preston)

1. *Ancient Celtic Christian Monks*

1.1 Driving Across Ireland

"When Abba Macarius was in Egypt,
he left his cell; and when he got back,
he found a thief in the process of stealing
everything the monk owned.

After watching awhile,
Monk Macarius
began helping load the thief's donkey
with the stolen goods.

Leading the animal out to the road,
Macarius said:

'We brought nothing into the world.
The Lord gave and the Lord has taken away.
Blessed be the name of the Lord.'"

(Job 1:21)

-Sayings of the Desert Fathers

Visiting Ireland

It *never* snows in Ireland." That's what the white-haired, middle-aged Irishman smoking the pipe had answered us in Dublin, when we asked how much snow fell in Ireland each year.

My wife Linda and I were visiting during January, and had noticed how similar the climate was to our own weather in the Pacific Northwest. Everywhere we traveled, the land was well watered and green, with temperatures ranging between 40 and 60 degrees Fahrenheit.

In Oregon and Washington, two days of snow per year is about average. Usually, it is already melted and gone by 9 or 10 a.m. the next morning. Once every fifteen years or so, there is a cold snap where the temperature stays below freezing, and then the snow may actually remain on the ground for as long as a week or two.

Visiting Castles

We spent three days traveling across the entire island of Ireland, visiting the completely restored and furnished medieval Bunratty Castle near Shannon Airport, and the ruins of Blarney Castle in County Cork.

Blarney Castle is one of five ancestral castles built by the ancient McCarthy Clan, whose descendants today include my wife Linda. At Blarney Castle, we learned that Linda's ancestors escaped from the castle through a secret tunnel, on the day that Oliver Cromwell wheeled up cannons and began shelling it.

Ever since, this knowledge has made it extremely difficult for us to view Cromwell objectively (the Irish also are not big Cromwell fans).

No Deaths from Falling in Over 100 Years

Many tourists at the castle kiss the Blarney Stone. It is located far up on the inside of the outer wall, nearly four stories high, and the person kissing it has to be held upside down by a Castle Guide to be able reach it. This is not a very pleasant prospect if you suffer from vertigo at great heights.

It is a thirty-seven foot drop to the ground below. The Guide reassured tourists, pointing out that it had been over one hundred years since anyone had fallen to their death.

There is now a safety net in place about ten feet below the Stone.

1.2 Ireland's Western Coast

"He sends snow
like wool:
He scatters the frost
like ashes.

He casts forth His ice
like morsels:
who can stand before
His cold?"

-Psalm 147:16-17

Gale Force Winds

We finally arrived on the far western Atlantic Coast of Ireland, at the spectacularly steep and rugged Cliffs of Moher. We couldn't actually see Boston from this spot; but we knew that it was indeed out there somewhere, far over the horizon in the west.

The temperature had dropped suddenly to below freezing, and it was brutally cold, with gale-force winds. There were no other tourists in sight, but a local vendor had pulled up his van and set up a card table. It held discounted sweaters from the nearby Connemara Woolen Mills.

Connemara's Many Sweater Patterns

We bought two, putting them on immediately. The vendor drove away, for there was no one else there to sell to.

For many centuries, these sweaters had been hand-knitted by the wives of the local fishermen. Fishing from a small boat on the Atlantic Ocean has always been extremely dangerous, especially when a storm suddenly arises.

The many different styles of knitted patterns that the sweaters are available in, had been created by the fishermen's wives so they could identify the washed-up bodies of their husbands.

Innumerable Irish fishermen throughout history have been drowned at sea.

A Black Tower

Continuing our climb up the slope to the nearby tall, black medieval tower, we took care not to be blown over the cliff's edge by the extreme winds. Climbing the tower was a relief, for inside we were partially shielded from the wind, although it was still very, very cold.

This tower had been built by the O'Brien Clan, reminding me of several wonderful childhood visits to the Iowa dairy and popcorn farm of my O'Brien cousins.

Viking Raiders

The view of the immense gray, boiling Atlantic, was spectacular from the top of the dark tower. It was a watchtower, built to warn of the arrival of Viking raiders during the violent turbulence of the Middle Ages.

We left the spectacular Cliffs of Moher, driving our rental car, and continuing on our journey. This itself was quite an experience, for the entire country of Ireland drives on the "wrong" side of the road as far as Americans are concerned.

Driving Through A Blizzard

Heading south toward the Dingle Peninsula, we looked forward to reaching our destination: a colorful little seaside town on the Bay of Dingle, where we would be spending the night.

We had heard that a porpoise made its home in the bay. It had become a sort of town mascot, and followed the local boats around the bay.

There was only a small mountain range to cross over before we arrived. As we climbed the narrow, cliff-side roads, a blizzard struck, and visibility was reduced to a few feet in front of us. It was a long, harrowing, and seemingly endless drive ever upward. With great relief we found ourselves suddenly emerging above the clouds, and above the snowstorm.

We stopped and rested on a beautiful alpine pass, breaking out a delicious lunch before descending the farther, snow-free side of the mountains, to the beautiful ocean bay far below us in the distance.

32

1.3 Visiting Monastery Ruins

"I have devoted my energies
to the study of the Scriptures,
observing monastic discipline,
and singing the daily services in church;

study, teaching, and writing
have always been my delight."

-The Venerable Bede (c. 672-735 A.D.)
Monk, England's First Historian
Author: *The Ecclesiastical History*
of the English People

Castles and Monasteries

The next few days we spent visiting monastic ruins. Seemingly every five miles in Ireland one discovers the ruins of a castle or monastery. The larger ruins date from the Middle Ages, and these monasteries were built in medieval times by the later Roman Catholic Orders.

In 1172 A.D., these continental monastic Orders replaced the earlier Celtic Christian Orders. Up until then, the Celtic Christian monastic Orders had flourished independently and autonomously in Ireland for 740 years, ever since the time of St. Patrick.

The Dingle Peninsula

We were interested especially in the earlier monastic ruins dating from the Celtic Christian era, and they are to be found everywhere, scattered throughout the Dingle Peninsula. Many of these were smaller monasteries, often consisting of as few as twelve monks.

Generally, they would have a small stone Oratory (a Chapel in which the Gospel was read), small beehive-shaped stone huts in which the monks lived, and a circular wall built of stone surrounding the whole.

All were built using traditional drystone technique, a natural waterproofing technique, where many small stones of just the correct shape are placed together by hand; no mortar being used, or needed.

Field Stones

The Irish soil is completely saturated with stones, and to farm there you need to continually be removing them, as they keep working their way to the surface.

The easiest way to get them out of the way is to build stone walls completely around the fields with them, and that is what everyone has always done.

Peasants' cottages, pigsties, corrals, and pretty much everything else in Ireland has always been built from stone. Stones are found in abundance everywhere.

Mountains Named for Patrick and Brendan

It is from this far western portion of Ireland that St. Patrick began his missionary work throughout the island.

Here is the mountain that has been named for him: *Croagh Patrick*. In Irish Gaelic it is *Cruach Phadráig*. *Cruach* means *hill or mountain*.

Here too, on this scenic peninsula, is *Brandan's Mountain*, where St. Brendan's monastery was located, overlooking the Atlantic Ocean.

From this spot, Brendan the Navigator sailed to Scotland and Iceland, possibly to Greenland, and some have believed he may have explored even farther south, in continental North America.

432 A.D. - God Sends Patrick to Ireland

The *tradition* is that a Pope sent Patrick to evangelize Ireland, converting it to Roman Catholicism. The historical evidence is overwhelmingly otherwise.

St. Patrick, as stated by himself in his own writings, was called and sent directly *by God* in visions in three dreams, as a missionary to Ireland.

He converted the entire island of Ireland to a uniquely Celtic form of *Nicene* Christianity.

The year that Patrick arrived in Ireland and began proclaiming the Good News of Christ to the pagan Irish, followers of the Druid priests, is generally considered to be 432 A.D.

840 A.D. - Vikings Founded the City of Dublin

Because Ireland still had not yet developed cities, Christianity there was based around its monastic centers.

Vikings first began arriving from Norway and raiding its monasteries in 795 A.D. They began settling permanently in 840 A.D., founding Dublin, Ireland's very first town, as a trading center.

We visited Ireland's capital city of Dublin (in Gaelic *Duiblinn*, which means *Blackpool*). *Duiblinn* was the Irish name of the Lake where the Vikings chose to harbor their dragon ships.

We toured Dublin Castle, Ireland's "White House," where the President of Ireland lives. Viking ruins had been discovered beneath the castle, and were being excavated. We toured these, also.

The Muiredach Celtic High Cross

I wear a gold Celtic Cross necklace that is a scaled-down replica of the full-size, 17 foot tall, stone High Cross of Muiredach in Monasterboice, Ireland. The theme of the cross is *"Christ the King, Lord of the Earth,"* and it is covered with carvings of many Biblical scenes of Christ from the Gospels.

It is considered one of the most beautiful, perhaps *the* most beautiful of all the Celtic High Crosses. However, the reason I purchased it from the Gift Shop in Dublin Castle, is because it is a replica of the only High Cross I know of that has two cats carved on it.

My wife Linda loves cats.

At the bottom of the Muiredach Cross, one of the cats is kissing a bird, and the other is kissing a mouse. This was the monks' portrayal of the verse:

> *'The wolf also shall dwell with the lamb,*
> *and the leopard shall lie down*
> *with the young kid goat;*
> *and the calf, and the young lion,*
> *and the fattened calf together;*
>
> *and a little child shall lead them. "*

-Isaiah 11:6

1.4 God Sends Patrick to Ireland

"I am Patrick, yes, a sinner
and indeed untaught;
yet I am established
here in Ireland where I
profess myself Bishop.

I am certain in my heart
that all that I am,
I have received from God.

So I live among
barbarous tribes,
a stranger and an exile
for the love of God."

-St. Patrick (390-461 A.D.)

1172 A.D. - The Synod of Cashel

As mentioned earlier, the Celtic Christians of Ireland first came under Papal jurisdiction in 1172 A.D., at the Synod of Cashel, 740 years after Patrick began his ministry.

In 596 A.D., 135 years after Ireland had been converted by St. Patrick to Christianity, what the Roman Catholic Church calls *the first major mission of Rome*, the *Gregorian Mission*, was instigated by Pope Gregory the Great.

He sent Augustine of Canterbury as a Missionary to southern Britain to convert the pagan Anglo-Saxon tribes to Christ.

These barbarian hordes had invaded Britain in regular waves after the departure of the Romans in 410 A.D.

Of course, there had already been Christians; both Romans and converted native Britons; living in Britain for nearly 400 years, following the Roman conquest of Britain in 43 A.D.

St. Patrick's family was among these.

Patrick evangelized Ireland until his death on March 17, 461 A.D.

S.G. Preston

The Pentarchy

In the Early Church, authority was held mutually by the Patriarchs of the five major Episcopal Sees. These were: Jerusalem, Antioch, Rome, Alexandria, and lastly, in the 4th century, Constantinople was added. Moscow did not become a Sixth Patriarchate among the Orthodox Communions until 1589.

The ancient five Sees of the Early Church were collectively known as the *Pentarchy* (Greek, meaning: *five rule*), and received legal status under the Emperor Justinian I (527-565 A.D.). The Patriarch of the Episcopal See of Rome is better known in the West by two other of his titles: Bishop of Rome, and Pope. The Papacy's claim of absolute (Judicial) authority over all Christians can be traced at least as far back as Pope Leo I. Leo I (the Great) was Pope from 440-461 A.D.

1042 A.D. - The Great Schism

It was not until nearly 600 years later, in the 11th century, that a Bishop of Rome first attempted to *enforce* the doctrine of Papal Judicial Primacy -- upon the Orthodox Churches in Italy that looked to the See of Constantinople as their spiritual authority, not to Rome.

In 1996, Jesuit Historian Klaus Schatz S.J., in his book, *Papal Primacy: From its Origins to the Present* (P. 3) wrote:

> *"If one had asked a Christian in the year 100, 200, or even 300*
> *whether the Bishop of Rome was the head of all Christians,*
> *or whether there was a supreme bishop over all the other bishops*
> *and having the last word in questions affecting the whole Church,*
> *he or she would certainly have said no."*

This doctrine of *Primacy*, along with the Roman addition to the universal Christian Creed (the *Nicene Creed*) of the *"filioque"* clause (Latin: *"and the Son"*) was the primary cause of The Great Schism: the separation of the See of Rome from the other four ancient Episcopal Sees.

These four Sees, Jerusalem being the oldest, and Antioch the second oldest, are collectively known as the Orthodox Christian Church, and generally referred to by scholars and others as *Eastern Orthodoxy*.

41

The See of Antioch

Antioch holds a unique distinction in the New Testament:

"And the disciples were first called Christians in Antioch."

-Acts 11:26

The See of Antioch makes the claim to have been founded by the Apostle Peter, seven years *before* he journeyed to Rome. This is attested to by Eusebius of Caesarea, Origen, St. Jerome, St. John Chrysostom, Pope Gelasius, and others.

Peter's arrival in Antioch before he went to Rome is even mentioned in the New Testament in Galatians 2:11-21. This is where Peter's altercation with the Apostle Paul is recorded.

1155 A.D. – The Laudabiliter

In 1155 A.D., Pope Adrian IV, the only Englishman to serve in that office, granted authority in a Papal Bull (an official Church document), to King Henry II of England to effect the conquest of Ireland.

The Document is known as *The Laudabiliter,* from its first words in Latin. Henry's conquest was accomplished sixteen years later, in 1171 A.D. The Papal Bull states that this authority was granted specifically:

"...for the enlarging of the bounds of the Church."

This indicates that Pope Adrian himself acknowledged that the Celtic Christians of Ireland were not a part of the Roman Catholic Church.

The Church's official stance is that this particular Papal Bull cannot be genuine. The idea that a Pope would order Ireland's conquest and forcible conversion to Catholicism (...and by England!) would not be not be very good public relations in Ireland.

No actual copy of the document is in existence today. However, scholars cite many references to it in other historical documents in several different countries, and dating as far back as the 13th century.

Charlemagne

The farmer's ancestor had no doubt thought that the beehive-shaped huts, built by those monks of long ago, provided a nice covered area where his sows could take shelter from the Irish rain.

It was truly awe-inspiring to think that when ancient Celtic monks were living in these very same stone huts, Byzantium still had a resident Roman Emperor, and Charlemagne was newly ascended to his throne.

1.7 *Skellig Michael*: The Monastery "Halfway to Heaven"

"For daily I expect to be murdered or betrayed
or reduced to slavery if the occasion arises.
But I fear nothing, because of the promises of Heaven;
for I have cast myself into the hands of God,
who reigns everywhere."

"If I have any worth, it is to live my life for God."

-St Patrick (390-461 A.D.)

———

"An rud is annamh is iontach."

"The thing that's seldom is wonderful."

-Old Gaelic Saying

A Rock in the Sea

Off this far western coast, but somewhat more toward the south of us, lay the island of *Skellig Michael*, an enormous mountain of rock rising steeply out of the ocean.

Skellig Michael is actually the westernmost part of the Republic of Ireland. It was inhabited by Irish Celtic monks for over 600 years, from 588-1222 A.D. Vikings attacked in 823 A.D., and again in 838 A.D.

Star Wars

Skellig (from the Gaelic *skeilic*, meaning *a rock in the sea*) is a Gaelic word used to describe a rock island out in the ocean. In ancient times, many high places were named after the Archangel Michael. *Mont Saint-Michel* in Normandy is another example.

You may have seen the *Star Wars* movies where Rey visits the older Luke Skywalker: *The Force Awakens* (2015), and *The Last Jedi* (2017). If you have, you may already know that the bizarre island shown in the film is not an artificial Hollywood creation. It is a very real place on this earth called *Skellig Michael*.

588 A.D. - Founded by Monk Fionán

There is an excellent secular historical work that chronicles the entire history of these most hardcore of Irish Celtic Christian monks, who lived on this strange rock:

Sun Dancing:
Life in a Medieval Irish Monastery
and How Celtic Spirituality
Influenced the World
by Geoffrey Moorhouse

The monastery on *Skellig Michael* was founded by Fionán, believed to be one of the original Brothers of the community of the voyaging monk, Brendan the Navigator.

As many other Celtic monks had done, they left in a boat with no sail or oars, to drift to the site of their new monastery, wherever God would take them; facing possible death if they were carried out into the open ocean.

George Bernard Shaw

On September 18, 1910, George Bernard Shaw wrote in a letter to a friend, a description of his recent visit by fishing boat to the island:

"...they landed me on the most fantastic
and impossible rock in the world:

Skellig Michael,
or the Great Skellig,
where in southwest gales
the spray knocks stones out of the
lighthouse keeper's house,
160 feet above calm sea level.

There is a Little Skellig,
covered with gannets...
both the Skelligs are pinnacled,
crocketed, spired, arched,

caverned, minaretted;
and these gothic extravagances
are not curiosities
of the islands;
there is nothing else.

The rest of the cathedral
may be under the sea for all I know:
there are 90 fathoms by the chart,
out of which the Great Skellig
rushes up 700 feet so suddenly
that you have to go
straight up stairs to the top –
over 600 steps.

And at the top,
amazing beehives
of flat rubble stones,
each overlapping the one below
until the circle meets in a dome --
cells, oratories, churches,
and outside them cemeteries,
wells, crosses,
all clustering like shells
on a prodigious rock pinnacle,
with precipices
sheer down on every hand,
and lodged on the projecting stones
overhanging the deep huge stone coffins
made apparently by giants,
and dropped there
God knows how.

An incredible, impossible, mad place...
I tell you the thing does not belong
to any world that you and I
have lived and worked in:

it is part of our dream world...
I hardly feel real again yet."

Charlemagne

In the late eighth through the early ninth century, the Holy Roman Emperor Charlemagne would "import" monks from Ireland.

They were the only Europeans of his time, outside of Byzantium, who still knew how to read and write.

Charlemagne would assign one monk to himself and one to each of the nobility, so that the leaders of his empire could communicate with each other.

Messengers would deliver notes hand-written in Latin, from the first monk to another stationed at the other end of the line, who would then read it and translate the message to *his* noble.

The additional duties of these monks consisted of founding and running schools to educate the citizens of the empire. This was the beginning of what would later be known as the *Carolingian Renaissance*.

Sir Kenneth Clark

No less an authority than the historian Sir Kenneth Clark once stated:

> *"It was in places
> like Skellig Michael
> that Western Civilization
> was preserved."*

Answers to Prayer
PrayerFoundation ™ 24-Hr. Prayerchain

Sept. 11, 2004 - Prayer Request:

Please pray for native missionary Pastor Manrathan and his wife, and for Bible Distributor Sarita.

These folks are Indian Nationals who work with *Gospel For Asia*. The pastor and his wife have been captured, beaten and threatened with death. Sarita is also being held hostage.

The group responsible is the same one that burned alive missionary Graham Staines and his children, a few years ago.

Thank you.

Doug (Ontario, Canada)

Answer to Prayer - Sept. 16, 2004 (5 Days Later)

Praise God! A good report out of India! Native missionary Pastor Manrathan and his wife, and Bible lady Sarita, have all been released from bondage.

Though all three were beaten before their release, they have all been returned safe. There is no evidence of the ransom being paid.

Upon hearing of this persecution, seventeen other native pastors had gone to the village and spoke with each of the hostage takers.

Though they were met with hostility, they watched as the Spirit of God softened hearts, and within a short time, the decision was made to release the captives.

-Doug (Ontario, Canada)

(From the book: *Answers to Prayer* by S.G. Preston)

2. Celtic Christian Missionary Monks

2.1 Monk Ninian of Scotland

"...the southern Picts received the true faith
by the preaching of Bishop Ninias,
a most reverend and holy man
of the British nation...

whose Episcopal See,
named after St. Martin the Bishop,
and famous for a church dedicated to him
(wherein Ninias himself
and many other saints rest in the body),
is now in the possession of the English nation.

The place belongs to the province
of the Bernicians and is commonly called
the White House (Candida Casa),
because he there built a church of stone,
which was not usual
amongst the Britons."

-The Venerable Bede (Writing c. 731 A.D.)
Author: *The Ecclesiastical History*
of the English People

Ninian, Bede, and Martin of Tours

The earliest account of Ninian (or: *Ninias*) is found in The Venerable Bede's masterwork: *The Ecclesiastical History of the English People*. The facts given in the passage above are practically all we know about St. Ninian's life and work.

Ninian is believed to have come from the Solway region in southwest Scotland (Roman *Caledonia*). He became a monk and studied at Martin of Tours' Marmoutier monastery in Gaul.

Returning in 397 A.D. as the first Christian missionary to his homeland, with the help of masons from the Marmoutier monastery, Ninian built the first church in Scotland.

397 A.D. - Hwit Aerne

Around this church grew up the first Christian settlement north of Hadrian's Wall; the wall between England and Scotland, which marked the northernmost border of the Roman Empire. It would be only thirteen more years until the Romans completely withdrew from Britain, in 410 A.D.

Ninian's church was said to be a whitewashed stone building, which could be easily seen from a distance. Most churches in Britain at this time were still made of wood.

In the language of the local Picts *White House* was translated as *Hwit Aerne*. Over time it became known as *Whithorn*. Its daughter house in Wales was called *Ty Gwynn*, the *Bright House*.

Ninian and Columba Evangelize Scotland

Ninian converted the Southern Picts, half of Scotland, to Christ. The other half, the Northern Picts, would not be converted until 100 years later, by an Irish monk named Columba. In Ireland, he is better known by his nickname: *Columcille*.

During the time of Ninian, there weren't yet any monks in Ireland, the Irish were still a pagan people, and their religious life was ruled entirely by Druids.

As Christianity, which the Celtic peoples simply called *The Faith*, continued its spread across the world, the situation in Ireland was about to change.

403-406 A.D. - Patrick Kidnapped

Sometime between 403 and 406 A.D., a young man named Patrick, sixteen years old and living on the coast of Britain, was kidnapped by Irish pirates, taken to Ireland, and sold into slavery.

The life of this *one* man would be used by God to completely change an entire nation; to completely change an entire people. But there were still a few impediments to be worked out.

First, Patrick would need to become a Christian. And even before that, he would need to believe that there was a God.

2.2 Patrick Captured by Slave Raiders

*"Nitear carn morde
chlachan beagga."*

*"A big cairn is made up
of little stones."*

-Old Gaelic Proverb

———

*"I pray to God
to give me perseverance
and to deign that I
be a faithful witness to Him
to the end of my life
for God."*

-St Patrick (390-461 A.D.)

Kidnapped and Enslaved

What is unusual about St. Patrick compared to others of his time period, is that much of what we know about Patrick comes from his own writings.

The young *Patricius* was raised in a Roman home on the west coast of Britain. It was a Christian home, but Patrick was not interested in Christianity.

He states in his writings that at that time he didn't even believe in God.

Patrick was captured by Irish slave raiders and taken to *Hibernia* (the Roman name for Ireland), where he served in slavery as a shepherd.

Ill clad, cold, and hungry, he finally gave his life to Christ.

Now he prayed all day long. After six long years, he heard a voice saying:

*"Your hungers are rewarded;
you are going home.
Look: your ship is ready."*

Escaping Ireland

Patrick started walking, traveling over two hundred miles. Amazingly, since he was a runaway slave, he was not stopped, or even questioned. Patrick wrote about this incident in his *Confession*:

"I came in God's strength...and had nothing to fear."

When Patrick finally reached the southeastern Irish coast, he saw a ship, and asked to go with those sailing it, but was refused.

He went off a short way, prayed, and then heard one of the sailors calling out that they had changed their minds; he could come with them after all.

The ship sailed to the European continent, but eventually Patrick was able to make his way home to his family and friends in Britain.

2.3 Monk Patrick of Ireland

"In essentials unity.
In non-essentials liberty.
In all things love."

-Rupertus Meldenius (1582-1651)
Lutheran Theologian

c. 410 A.D. – Honoratus Founds Lérins Monastery

One of Patrick's childhood friends heard about the new movement of Christian Monasticism, and the brand new monastery of Lérins Abbey.

It was located on one of the Lérins Islands off the coast of southern France.

The monastery had been founded just a few years before, sometime around 410 A.D., by Honoratus of Lérins (or: Arles; 350-429 A.D.; in French: St. Honore).

He had served as Archbishop of Amiens, and became the founder and first Abbot of Lérins Abbey.

Note: Remember that 410 A.D. is the year the Romans withdrew from Britain. The Roman Empire was shrinking, and Christianity was expanding.

Honoratus Seeks Solitude

Honoratus was born into a Consular Gallo-Roman family, and had converted from paganism to Christianity in his youth.

After his ministry as an Archbishop, he went to live in solitude on the Lérins island that would later be named for him.

To this day it is known as *Ile Saint-Honorat*. Others joined him, and he organized them into a monastic community. There have been monks living continuously at Lérins ever since Honoratus settled there as a solitary hermit monk.

The current monastery was built beginning in 1073 A.D., and today is home to a community of Cistercians.

John Cassian, Lérins Monastery, & Benedict of Nursia

The monk John Cassian (360-435 A.D.) had close ties with the monastery at Lerins, and thought highly of it. Two of his books: *The Institutes* and *The Conferences*, record the monastic teachings of the Desert Fathers.

The practices of these monks living in the Egyptian desert, who Cassian had visited and interviewed, helped disperse monastic teaching throughout the west. St. John Cassian's teachings were later spread by Benedict of Nursia (480-543 A.D.), who praised *The Conferences* in his Rule: *The Rule of Saint Benedict*.

Question:

But why did Patrick have to go so far away from his home in Britain, all the way to what is now southern France, just to find a monastery?

Answer:

There were *no* monasteries yet in Britain. The Province of Gaul may have had as many as *four*, all recently founded. Lérins was the only one of these on an island off the coast. In ancient times, it was often much easier, quicker, cheaper, and less dangerous to travel by boat, rather than overland.

Patrick's friend decided to go to the Lérins Islands to learn about God. He told Patrick, who had recently returned home, all about the new monastery there. Patrick too, couldn't wait to move to Lérins Abbey and become a monk.

Patrick at Lérins

These are some of the things we know about St. Patrick's early life. Born between 387 and 390 A.D., Patrick was enslaved by Irish raiders at age sixteen: 403-406 A.D.

He escaped Ireland six years later, and returned to Britain at age 22; or perhaps age 23, if he did not return immediately.

Patrick left home to train for the priesthood and live the life of a monk in Gaul at the new Lérins Islands monastery, beginning in 412-414 A.D.

S.G. Preston

No Coherent History of St. Patrick

Unfortunately, Patrick's dates are somewhat fluid, and seemingly impossible to fit together. Most historians agree that he studied at Honoratus' Lérins Islands monastery, but the monastery at Auxerre, founded in 422 A.D., also claims him.

Searching everywhere, I could find no timeline that reconciled all of the known events, and many scholars claimed it was impossible to fit them together; that much of the information contradicted each other, especially as to the dates.

Like trying to solve a puzzle, I spent three days trying as many of the various combinations that I could come up with, to see if there was any way of reconciling *all* of the known information into one consistent chronology. I finally ended up with the following possible solution:

Timeline of St. Patrick's Life

Patrick born in 390 A.D.;
enslaved in 406 A.D.;
escaped and returned to Britain in 412 A.D.

In France at Lérins Monastery,
(founded c. 410 A.D.), for ten years,
from 412 to 422 A.D.

(or a later start date by one or two years
if he remained in Britain longer,
or returned to Britain later.)

At Auxerre Monastery,
(founded 422 A.D.), also for ten years,
from 422 to 432 A.D.

Patrick was the Apostle to Ireland
as a Missionary Bishop
from 432-461 A.D.,
for 29 or 30 years.

He went home to be with the Lord
on March 17, 461 A.D.

2.4 St. Patrick's Legacy

"Give me one hundred preachers
who fear nothing but sin
and desire nothing but God,
and I care not a straw
whether they be clergy or laymen;
such alone will shake the gates of hell
and set up the kingdom of God on earth.

God does nothing but in answer
to prayer."

-John Wesley (1703-1791)
Anglican Priest
Founder: Methodists

Irish Monks Share the Gospel Throughout Europe

Ireland embraced Christianity through Patrick's ministry. There would soon be monks and monasteries everywhere throughout the length and breadth of the entire island.

In 563 A.D., 102 years after the death of St. Patrick, St. Columba, accompanied by 12 monks, would leave Ireland for the island of Iona off the southwest coast of Scotland. They founded a monastic community, and once settled in, began to convert the pagan Picts of northern Scotland to Christ.

Over the next few hundred years, thousands of other Irish *missionary monks* would follow Columba's example, and leave Ireland to preach the Gospel all across the European continent.

After the Empire

The Roman Empire began in 753 B.C. The Western Roman Empire had been overrun by numerous barbarian tribal peoples, including the Goths, Huns, Vandals, and Visigoths, and suffered final collapse in the West on September 4, 476 A.D.

This is the date on which the Germanic barbarian Odoacer began his rule by overthrowing Romulus, the last Roman Emperor in the West.

Arianism

The Byzantine Eastern Roman Empire would remain in existence for nearly 1,000 years longer, until conquered in 1453 by the Ottoman Turks.

Irish monks, who proliferated *after* Patrick, *because* of Patrick, would convert pagan northern Europe to Christianity, and re-convert southern Europe.

When Bishop Arius of Alexandria was exiled from the Roman Empire, he had taken his heretical teachings; denial of the Trinity and denial of the Deity of Christ; and gone as a missionary to the barbarian tribes.

He converted the Visigoth ruling class to his cult of Arianism.

This violent tribe was taught by Arius to hate orthodox Christians, and to kill them wherever they found them.

Parts of the Visigoth horde drove through Spain and North Africa, massacring Christians in an attempt to wipe them completely off the face of the earth.

Many European Cities Began as Irish Monasteries

When the Irish Celtic Christian monks arrived to evangelize Europe, it was a European continent populated by pagan barbarian hordes.

These included Huns, Goths, Vandals, and Visigoths: and the Visigoth ruling class consisted of Arian cultists hostile to orthodox Nicene Christianity.

Celtic Christian monks would lead many to Christ.

They would preserve the lost arts, in the West, of reading and writing. Copying each individual manuscript by hand; along with the Scribes of Byzantium in the East; they would preserve the Bible for all future generations.

Irish monks would also establish monasteries all across Europe. Over twenty of these of these Celtic Christian monasteries grew up into well-known European cities.

These include Trier, Auxerre, St. Gall, Regensburg, Wurzburg, Reichenau, Taranto, Salzburg, and Vienna.

The Film: The Sound of Music

Salzburg, Austria, is famous as the birthplace of Wolfgang Amadeus Mozart.

I remember that when Linda and I were visiting the monastery grounds there, we were shown where different parts of the movie *The Sound of Music* had been filmed, in the very places where the events had actually taken place in real life.

The caves high up in the cliff wall were pointed out to us. Here the original Irish Celtic monks had first settled and lived, when the entire area was still an uninhabited wilderness.

Irish monks even founded an Irish Celtic Christian monastery in Bobbio, Italy. It is located in the north of Italy, near the Apennine Mountains.

The monastery in Bobbio is still there, and if you are ever in the area of Milan, you can visit it.

The Book: How the Irish Saved Civilization

The story of Patrick and the thousands of monk-robe wearing ancient Irish "Billy Grahams" journeying to Scotland, northern England, and continental Europe with the message of Christ, is beautifully told in the second half of the book:

How the Irish Saved Civilization
by Thomas Cahill

This is a secular historical work, not a Christian one.

We recommend beginning reading in the middle of the book, with what we consider to be the best Chapter on St. Patrick ever written, and completely skipping the entire unedifying first half of the book, about pre-Christian pagan Ireland.

2.5 Brendan the Navigator's First Voyage

*"Those who sail
on the sea in ships,
who do business
in great waters;*

*these see the works
of the LORD,
and His wonders
in the deep."*

-Psalm 107:23-24

Erc of Slane, Ita of Killeedy, & Brigid of Kildare

Brendan the Navigator was born near Tralee, in County Kerry, Ireland. At the age of one year, he was given into the care of St. Ita of Killeedy, who had founded a Convent there. She would become one of the most famous female monastics in the history of Ireland.

Another of Brendan's teachers was Bishop Erc of Slane. He was still a Druid priest, when he first met St. Patrick.

Giant bonfires were lit to announce the pagan festivals. St. Patrick lit a giant bonfire to announce Christianity's arrival, before preaching to King Laoghaire and his Druids at the Hill of Slane in 433 A.D.

Erc mac Dega was the only one of these Druid priests to pay homage to Patrick at that meeting. He was later converted to Christ by Patrick, who appointed Erc to be the first Bishop of Slane.

Patrick sent Bishop Erc as a *missionary Bishop* to Kerry, to complete its evangelization. Sometime before 461 A.D., Patrick had sent Erc to evangelize Munster. Erc returned there to evangelize with Brigid of Kildare in 484 A.D. St. Erc founded a Monastery at Slane that would survive for 600 years.

He later journeyed to Cornwall, and is honored as a Cornish saint there. Eventually, Erc returned to live in a Hermitage at Slane, where he devoted his final years to prayer.

Brendan Founds Monasteries

In 512 A.D., Bishop Erc became the six year-old Brendan's tutor for two years. Erc went home to be with the Lord at the age of 93, in 514 A.D.

Brendan was later allowed to fulfill his desire to travel to, and study with, many different holy men and women.

At an early age, Brendan began attracting disciples and founding monasteries. These were places of public worship, with Christian schools and education. Today we call this *"church planting."*

Clonfert is the most famous of Brendan's monasteries, founded in 560 A.D. At its peak, Clonfert Monastery was home to 3,000 monks.

It remained in existence as a school until the 1600's.

Brendan Meets Columba

Brendan's first voyage took him to the Arran Islands off Scotland (spelled with two "r's"), and not to be confused with the Aran Islands (spelled with only one "r") that are located off the western Irish coast, just north of the Cliffs of Moher.

While in the Scottish Arran Islands, Brendan founded another monastery.

He then continued on to visit many other islands, including Hynba Island off the coast of Scotland, where Brendan is said to have met Columba. Adomnan also records a visit of Brendan to Columba at Iona.

On this first voyage, Brendan also traveled to Wales, and finally to Brittany, on the northern coast of France.

Many places in Ireland are named after Brendan.

The most famous is Mount Brandon, where Brendan had founded a monastery, and where he is said to have had his vision of a far-off island.

2.6 Monk Brendan's Second Voyage

"Unfurl the sails,
and let God steer us
where He will."

-The Venerable Bede
Monk, Historian (672/73-735 A.D.)
Author: *The Ecclesiastical History*
of the English People

Seven-Year Voyage

It is Brendan's second voyage for which he is most well-known. Brendan and the monks that went with him are said to have fasted for forty days and then left on a seven-year sea journey. Some believe that the monks even reached Iceland and Greenland.

When the Norwegian Viking known as Eric the Red "discovered" Iceland, he found Irish monks already living there!

The monks didn't care much for their new neighbors, or for their loss of solitude, and soon left.

Some think Brendan may even have sailed to North America. Brendan spoke of discovering a new island far to the west.

This might have been Greenland.

The new island was placed on many of the world maps made from that time on, and may have been one of the influences for Christopher Columbus' voyages.

1975 – An Irish Coracle Sails Across the Atlantic

I remember when *National Geographic Magazine* covered the story of adventurer Tim Severin.

In 1975 he sailed a traditional wood and leather Irish coracle across the Atlantic.

His idea was to show that Brendan could in fact have reached America in an ancient Irish boat.

Medieval Bestseller

The voyages of Monk Brendan were first recorded for posterity by The Venerable Bede. In the ninth century, another Irish monk wrote the book: *Navigatio Sancti Brendani* (*Voyage of St. Brendan*).

This became one of the most popular books of the Middle Ages, making Brendan famous throughout Europe as a voyager.

The book was written as an allegory, so it is difficult to identify the specific places described in it.

For example, Brendan is said to have come upon a "mountain of glass" floating in the ocean. This sounds completely fanciful, until one realizes that probably an iceberg is what is being referred to.

A small "moving, sinking island" is believed to be a whale.

Brendan went home to be with the Lord in 578 A.D., from the town of Annaghdown, Ireland.

* * *

C.S. Lewis, C. Spurgeon, T. à Kempis, & Abba Pambo

"One of the purposes for which God instituted prayer may have been to bear witness that the course of events is not governed like a state, but created like a work of art to which every being makes a conscious contribution, and in which every being is both a means and an end."

-C.S. Lewis (1898-1963)

———

"O that Christ crucified were the universal burden of men of God. Your guess at the number of the Beast... your conjectures concerning a personal Antichrist – forgive me, I count them but mere bones for dogs; while men are dying, and Hell is filling, it seems to me the veriest drivel to be muttering about an Armageddon... I would sooner pluck one single brand from the burning than explain all mysteries."

-Charles Spurgeon (1834-1892)

———

"The religious who meditates devoutly on the most holy life and passion of our Lord will find all that he needs to make his life worthwhile. In fact, he has no need to go beyond Jesus, for he will discover nothing better."
"Hold fast to Jesus both in life and in death and commit yourself to His steadfast love, for He alone can help you when all others fail."

-Thomas à Kempis (1380-1471) From: *The Imitation of Christ*

———

"God is the source of life for all humanity. He has given Christ, the Way of Salvation; available to all.
"If you have a heart, you can be saved."'

-Abba Pambo (305-375 A.D.) *Sayings of the Desert Fathers*

Answers to Prayer

PrayerFoundation ™ 24-Hr. Prayerchain

Oct. 20, 2002 - Answer to Prayer

You prayed for my friend G., who had a mastectomy almost a year ago.

Because of her lupus, she was not able to have Chemo. She did have Radiotherapy in Dec./Jan. and suffered for nearly six months afterwards with burning, lumps/boils/abscesses, and extreme tiredness. They normally give iodine to alleviate these symptoms, but she is allergic to iodine, and so couldn't be given it.

She visited her Oncologist in August, and he said she is fine. Praise the Lord!

Many thanks!

-Sophia (Israel)

_____

(From the book: *Answers to Prayer* by S.G. Preston)

3. *Celtic Monks Evangelize Europe*

3.1 Noon: Psalm 23

"Agus beimid inar n-aoiri,
ar do shonsa,
a Thiarna, ar do shonsa.

Ta cumhacht tagtha anuas o do lamh,
ionas go gcomhlionadh
ar gcosa do thoil go tapaidh.

Srithoimid ar aghaidh
mar abhainn chugat,
Agus plodaithe le hanamacha
a bheid si go deo."

"And shepherds we shall be,
for Thee my Lord, for Thee.

Power hath descended forth from Thy hand,
so our feet may swiftly
carry out Thy command.

And we shall flow a river forth to Thee,
and teeming with souls shall it ever be."

-Old Gaelic Hymn

Darkness Covered the Land

Now it is Noon. I kneel in the Chapel on the enormous red Persian carpet and pray the 23rd Psalm, as I do every day at this time when I am here:

"The LORD is my shepherd;
I shall not want.
He maketh me to lie down
in green pastures.
He leadeth me
beside the still waters..."

Peter's Vision

The Apostle Peter was also praying at Noon, when he had the vision that would convince the Apostles to allow Gentiles to become members of the Christian community.

The Bible records that Peter:

> *"...saw heaven opened,*
> *and something like*
> *a large sheet descending..."*

-Acts 10:11

This is also the time during Christ's Crucifixion when darkness covered the land, beginning at *"the sixth hour,"* noon, and remaining until *"the ninth hour,"* 3 p.m. (Luke 23:44).

3.2 Monk Columba of Iona

"That man is little to be envied,
whose patriotism would not gain force
upon the plain of Marathon,

or whose piety would not grow warmer
among the ruins of Iona."

-Dr. Samuel Johnson (1709-1784)
Visiting the island of Iona in 1773

Illuminated Manuscripts

Columba (521-597 A.D.) is the Latinized name of the Irish monk who founded the Celtic monastery on Iona, an island off the coast of southwest Scotland, and converted the pagan Northern Picts to Christ.

Columba was born 60 years after the death of St. Patrick. The illuminated manuscript, *The Book of Kells,* was created in one of the monasteries that Columba founded. It was kept for centuries in the monastery at Kells, Ireland.

It is considered to be the most beautiful of all the many Gospels that were Illuminated (decorated with artwork) in Celtic Christian monasteries. The original manuscript is kept under glass in the library at Trinity College in Dublin. Linda and I were blessed to be able to view it there.

One of the Best Book Copyists

Born into the Irish royal family in 521 A.D., Columba's name in Gaelic is *Colum*, meaning: *dove.* Columba is the Latin rendering of his name. In Ireland, he has always been better known as *Columcille.* In Irish Gaelic, *Colum Cille* means: *dove of the church.*

Like The Venerable Bede, at a very young age Columba was placed in a monastery. There Columba became one of the best Scribes of his era. He is said to have personally created copies of over 300 books during his lifetime. One of his works is the illuminated *Book of Durrow*, which Linda and I also saw at Trinity College.

71

Founding Monasteries and Preaching the Gospel

Columba founded nearly one hundred monasteries in Ireland, including those at Derry, Durrow, and Kells.

At the age of 44, Columba left Ireland. Sometime around 563-565 A.D., he founded the monastery on the Scottish island of Iona.

It became his missionary base, from which he would bring Christianity to the pagan Picts of northern Scotland. Iona would also become the place where the Kings of Scotland received final interment.

Even the historical King Macbeth is buried there.

3.3 Columba's Mission to Scotland's Picts

"Dearly beloved, avenge not yourselves,
but rather give place unto wrath:
for it is written:

'Vengeance is mine; I will repay,'
saith the Lord."

-Romans 12:19

———

"A young monk took what an older monk
said to him as an insult.

The offended monk decided that he
wanted revenge on the other.

The younger monk complained to Abba Sisois
about what had happened.

'I will get back at him, Abba,'
the young monk declared.

Monk Sisois told the offended monk
that he should turn it over to God.

'Never!' the Brother said in anger.
'I'll never be satisfied until he pays for his words!'

Monk Sisois stood, and raised his hands.
He prayed: 'Lord, we no longer need you.

We find both You and your caring for us
to be totally unnecessary.

As this Brother says, we are quite well able
to avenge ourselves.'

The angry monk was shamed by these words.

He told Monk Sisois that he repented,
and would no longer seek revenge
on the other Brother."

-Sayings of the Desert Fathers

Taking the Gospel to a Pagan Nation

One hundred years after the monastery on Iona was founded, its ninth Abbot, Adomnan, would write a book called: *The Life of St. Columba.* Unfortunately, it is a very legendary and fanciful book, and contains little real information about Columba. For these reasons, we do not recommend reading it.

Why did Columba leave Ireland?

The Psalter

A reason given by some, but one which is very doubtful, because it didn't appear in the records until much later, is the Battle of Cooldrevny, resulting in 3,000 deaths. It comes in several versions.

One version claims that Columba had copied a *Psalter (Book of Psalms)* without permission, and was ordered to give up the copy that he had made. When he refused, his relatives sided with him, and the *Battle of Cooldrevny* was fought.

Wrongful Prayer Against the Enemy

Another version contends that during the battle, Columba prayed against those who fought against his relatives, and these suffered the majority of the casualties.

In all of the later alternate versions, Columba was either banished from Ireland, or banished himself, until he should convert as many pagans to Christ as the number of the three thousand warriors who were killed in the battle.

A Desire to Win Souls for Christ

Even in all of these different accounts, the salvation of the lost was Columba's motivation to go to Scotland. Abbot Adomnan simply records that Columba left Ireland because of:

> *"...a desire to carry the Gospel*
> *to a pagan nation*
> *and win souls to God."*

Missionary Outreach

We think that this reason is probably the most accurate one given, because Columba's Iona *mission monastery* would ultimately convert the Northern Picts, half of Scotland, to Christ.

The contemplative prayer life of Columba and many other Celtic monks led to intense *missionary activity*.

The Celtic Christians found no contradiction in this. After all, the Celtic monks were simply *imitating Christ and the Apostles*.

These had prayed, and they had also preached the word of God. Where was the conflict?

A young man named Francis from Assisi, Italy would later come to the same conclusion.

3.4 Columba, Druids, & A White Horse

"Rud nach cluin
cluas cha
ghluais cridhe."

"That which the ear
doesn't hear
won't stir the heart."

-Old Gaelic Saying

Presenting Druids with Christ

Not long after establishing the monastery on Iona, Columba was preaching the Gospel on his way to Inverness, to witness to the pagan Pictish King Brude.

He was stopped by a group of Druids, who demanded that Columba and his twelve monks return to Ireland.

These pagan priests claimed that Druidism was the true religion, and drew a circle on the ground, saying that Christ was in conflict with the cycle of nature. Columba took his staff and drew an intersecting cross within the circle.

Christ the Creator

Columba then pointed out to the Druids that Christ could not be in conflict with nature because Christ, as the Second Person of the Trinity, had Himself *created* nature, and instead *complemented* nature; working with it and through it:

"All things were made through Him,
and without Him was not anything made,
that was made."

-John 1:3

This is one of several stories that are also used to explain the origin of the Celtic Cross.

Founding Monasteries to Convert Scotland

Later, when Iona grew, wherever Columba preached to the Picts, he would leave behind twelve monks, founding a new monastery.

The monastery would become a Mission Station and a center of Christian teaching, and eventually a Christian town would grow up around it.

Though Druid priests constantly opposed him, little by little the light of Christ shone in northern Scotland.

The White Horse

Adomnan also records a story about Columba and a white horse. Columba was 77 years old, and it is said that he was aware of his quickly approaching death.

In fact, he went home to be with the Lord that very week.

Columba was very tired, and sat down to rest. The loyal work-horse that carried the milk pails from the *booley* (*cow pen*) to the monastery came over to Columba and rested his head against Columba.

Love for Animals

The servant who had been walking with the horse began to lead him away, but Columba said to let the horse be.

The old monk felt that the white horse could sense that he (Columba) was going to die, and wanted to comfort him, or perhaps just say good-bye.

This story illustrates Columba's great love for animals, and they for him.

3.5 Monk Columbanus' Mission to the Franks

*"For whoever shall call upon the name of the Lord
shall be saved.*

*How then shall they call on Him who
they have not believed in?*

*And how shall they believe in Him who they
have not heard of?*

And how shall they hear without a preacher?

And how shall they preach, unless they are sent?

*As it is written: 'How beautiful are the feet
of those that proclaim the good news of peace,
and bring glad tidings
of good things!'"*

-Romans 10:13-15

Becoming a Monk

Columbanus (543-615 A.D.) was born in West Leinster, Ireland. It is said that because he was so good-looking, many women tried to tempt him.

Desiring to avoid this and live a holy Christian life, he decided to become a monk.

He took the cowl at Lough Erne, where he was well known for his godliness and great learning. He composed a commentary on the *Psalms* while he was there.

Taking the Gospel to the Continent

At the age of forty, Columbanus felt God calling him to preach the Gospel in other countries. Sailing with twelve monks, he shared Christ first in Scotland, and then across England.

He desired to take the Gospel message to continental Europe.

Columbanus and his fellow monks decided to go to Gaul (today's France), to spread the Good News of Christ.

Frankish Territory

Around 585 A.D., they arrived in Frankish territory, which at that time included portions of modern-day France, Germany, and Switzerland.

The monks settled in the Vosges Mountains of what is now eastern France, in the ruins of an old Roman fortress. Remaining there for twenty years, they founded an additional two monasteries, as the number of monks who were drawn to their community became too many for one region.

Much of the area where they settled was ruled by pagan barbarians. What little remained of the Church was extremely corrupt. Neither the Priests nor the Bishops were at all interested in their duties of preaching the Gospel and teaching the people.

Solitude

Columbanus had a great reputation for holiness, zeal, and learning. People from all over France traveled to his monastery.

So many people were arriving and wanting to see Columbanus, that he went to live for several years in a hidden cave, with only a single messenger connecting him to his monasteries.

Love of Nature

It was here in the wilderness that Columbanus' typically Celtic love of nature and animals is seen.

There are stories about Columbanus involving a bear, wolves, birds, and a squirrel: the birds sitting on his shoulder, and the squirrel taking its rest in his monk cowl.

3.6 Columbanus' Mission to Germany, Switzerland, Italy

*"Nior dhun Dia doras riamh
nar oscail se ceann eile."*

*"God never closed one door
without opening another."*

-Old Gaelic Saying

Frankish Bishops

Columbanus' Celtic monasteries were experiencing phenomenal growth, with large numbers of monks arriving to enter them, and even greater numbers of visitors.

Envy, jealousy, and enmity in the Frankish Bishops grew.

The local clergy obtained the help of the Pope in an attempt to gain control over Columbanus, and over his three large monastic centers.

At the same time, the corrupt secular rulers in the area were not pleased at being told the errors of their ways.

They ordered Columbanus and his original twelve monks back to Ireland.

New Mission Fields

The Celtic monks were placed on a ship sailing to Ireland, but it was turned back to land by a great storm.

The Captain put them ashore, saying that he refused to carry them aboard his ship any longer.

Columbanus and his little band of monks immediately left for the mission fields of Germany and Switzerland. Of course, there were no countries with those names at this time.

These areas of forest and mountain were inhabited by idolatrous barbarian tribes called the Alemanni and the Suevi.

Columbanus preached in Neustria and at Metz, in what is now Germany.

Many of the People Accepted Christ

Columbanus and his brother monks also shared the Gospel near Lake Zurich, but they suffered much persecution, until they were driven away.

At Lake Constance they were warmly received, and many of the people there accepted Christ. They founded a new monastery.

A year later, however, the Irish monks again began to experience persecution.

625 A.D. - Italy

Columbanus left for Italy, arriving in 625 A.D. near Milan.

There he founded the monastery of Bobbio, and fought the Arian heresy with correct Biblical teaching.

If it seems odd that Celtic monks would feel called to the *mission field* of Italy, remember that the Italian peninsula had been overrun by pagan and Arian barbarian hordes.

At this time, the western Roman Empire had not existed for 150 years.

Pope Honorius

No doubt the Irish monks felt that a sound Gospel message was especially needed in Italy at this time.

In that same year of 625 A.D., Honorius had been elected to the Papal Office.

According to *The Catholic Encyclopedia* (Entry: *Pope Honorius* by I. J. Chapman), Pope Honorius I would be condemned as a heretic 55 years later.

This occurred in 680 A.D., by the decision of the Sixth General Council of the Church.

For Columbanus, however, the seemingly endless problems in Italy were not even to be considered when compared with the glories of Heaven.

Columbanus' message was ultimately one of joyous hope.

No Home On Earth

*"Let us,
who are on the way,
hasten home.*

*For our whole life
is like the journey
of a single day.*

*Our first duty
is to love nothing here;
but let us place
our affections above,
our desires above,
our wisdom above;*

*and let us seek
our home above.*

*For the fatherland
is where our Father is:*

*we have no home
on earth."*

3.7 Monk Aidan of Lindisfarne

"He cultivated peace and love, purity and humility.

He was above anger and greed,
and despised pride and conceit.

He set himself to keep
and teach the laws of God,
and was diligent in study
and in prayer...

I greatly admire all these things
about Aidan."

-The Venerable Bede
Monk, Historian (672/673-735 A.D.)
Author: *The Ecclesiastical History*
of the English People

Missionary to Northumbria

An Irishman named Aidan (600-651 A.D.) became a monk at Iona in 630 A.D., at the age of thirty. Five years later he was sent by Columba to share the Gospel with the pagan Angles of Northumbria, in northern England.

Our word *English* comes from the word: *Angle-ish*.

635 A.D. - Lindisfarne

We too, admire Aidan; his zeal for the lost, his humility, and his trust in God. Aidan was sent as a missionary to Northumbria after an earlier monk named Corman had given up, complaining that the Angles were too uncivilized and stubborn to be Christianized.

In 635 A.D., Aidan founded the monastery on *Lindisfarne*, also known as *Holy Island*. King Oswin of the Angles had studied as a young man at Iona, and been converted to Christ by the monks there, but his people were not Christians.

It was at Oswin's own request that first Corman, and then Aidan, would be sent to his kingdom.

Witness for Christ

From Lindisfarne, Aidan preached to the Angles throughout Northumbria. He was the Celtic *missionary monk* who brought northern England to Christ.

Aidan loved to talk to the pagan Angles about Jesus. He would not ride a horse, because it deprived him of opportunities to witness about Christ while he traveled.

He believed it was easier to talk to people when you were at their level.

The King's Horse

King Oswin gave Aidan an expensive horse. Aidan had not ridden very far before he gave the horse away to a poor person.

The King was very angry with Aidan for doing this. Aidan asked the King if a horse was more important to him than someone that Christ had died for.

The King repented and asked Aidan's forgiveness.

3.8 Monk Hilda of Whitby Abbey

"Is i an t-ailleantachd maise nam ban."

"Modesty is the beauty of women."

-Old Gaelic Saying

———

*"Amma Syncletica said,
'Some live in the mountains,
but they act like they are
living in the towns;
they are solitary,
but they live in the crowd
of their own thoughts.*

*Others live in solitude
in their own mind,
even when in a
crowded city.'"*

-Sayings of the Desert Mothers

Founder of a Renowned Celtic Christian Monastery

Hilda of Whitby (or: Hild; 614-680 A.D.), a female Celtic monastic, was encouraged by Aidan of Lindisfarne to found and become Abbess of her own *"Double Monastery"* (one for men and one for women, but located next to each other) in Northumbria.

She made her Whitby Abbey a center of learning, and was also a patroness of the arts. One of the monks of Whitby, named Caedmon, earned great fame as a poet. Hilda's monastery was of such renown, that it was chosen in 664 A.D. as the place where the Synod of Whitby would be held.

However, the decision of this Synod would be to place northern England and all of its Celtic Christians under the authority of the Bishop of Rome. This was the end of Celtic Christian independence and existence in England.

Celtic Monks Leave

Following the Synod of Whitby, the Irish Celtic Christian monks returned home to their monastic community on the island of Iona in Scotland, or to Ireland. This Synod is yet another historical proof that the Celtic Christians of Ireland were not a part of the Roman Catholic Church.

As previously mentioned, Celtic Christians in Ireland would retain their independence from Rome for another 500 years after the Synod of Whitby, until the military conquest of Ireland by English King Henry II, and the resulting Synod of Cashel in 1172 A.D.

Abbess of a "Double Monastery"

With the conclusion of the Synod of Whitby, Hilda's creative Celtic practices, and her contributions to the development of Christian religious life were lost.

Celtic style "Double Monasteries" like Hilda's, consisting of both men and women, were forbidden by the Church of Rome.

Women, even those with the ecclesiastical office of Abbess, were no longer allowed to have authority over men, as had been the case in Hilda's life, and had so often occurred among Celtic Christian believers throughout Ireland.

3.9 Monk Cuthbert of Lindisfarne

*"So great was Cuthbert's eloquence, so keen his desire
to drive home what he had begun to teach,
so bright the light of his angelic countenance..."*

-The Venerable Bede
Monk, Historian (672/673-735 A.D.)
Author: *The Ecclesiastical History
of the English People*

721 A.D. - Bede Writes About Cuthbert

One of the books written by The Venerable Bede was called *The Life and Miracles of St. Cuthbert, Bishop of Lindisfarne.* Cuthbert was born sometime around 634 A.D. in Northumbria. From the time he was a little boy, he shepherded sheep in the mountains near the monastery of Melrose Abbey.

He became a monk of Melrose at about age 17, in 651 A.D. While there, he was educated by Celtic Christian monks from Ireland. One of Bede's comments can be taken to imply that Cuthbert was not himself an ethnic Celt, although some dispute this.

If he was not, Cuthbert was certainly very Celtic in his outlook. Especially in his love of nature, and of animals.

St. Cuthbert and St. Francis

Many of the stories told about Cuthbert involve animals, including a story about an eagle and one involving several otters. Because of this, in northern England he is sometimes compared to St. Francis.

St. Francis has been made the Patron Saint of Ecology and the Patron Saint of Animals; Cuthbert is considered to be one of the world's very first wildlife conservationists.

Cuthbert was concerned with protecting the Eider duck. This duck is now also known as *"St. Cuthbert's Duck,"* and familiarly in Northumbria as *"Cuddy's Duck."* These ducks are often seen around Lindisfarne today. Cuthbert's efforts nearly 1,400 years ago to protect them, were very successful indeed!

Hermit Monk and Missionary Bishop

At one time in his life, in common with Martin of Tours, Francis of Assisi, and Brother Lawrence; Cuthbert had been a soldier. Later he became, at different times, both a *cenobitic* monastery monk, and an *eremitic* hermit monk.

Towards the end of his life, he also became a monastic *Missionary Bishop*, following the example that had been set by St. Patrick.

Cuthbert had retired to the island of Inner Farne as a hermit monk, where he was happy to have only seals, seabirds, and God for company; but in 685 A.D., he was made Bishop of Lindisfarne.

685-687 A.D. - Two Years of Evangelism

The "Holy Island" was still home to the island monastery that Columba had sent Aidan to found.

While at Lindisfarne, Cuthbert's primary concern was with evangelizing the people of England who had still not received Jesus as their Lord and Savior.

Cuthbert traveled much, preaching everywhere with great energy.

After two years of sharing the Good News and converting many to Christ, he retired again to his island hermitage. In that same year of 687 A.D., he went home to be with the Lord.

Cuthbert's body was returned to Lindisfarne for burial, as had been his desire.

* * *

Billy Graham On Prayer

"Prayer is crucial in evangelism:
Only God can change the heart of someone
who is in rebellion against Him.

No matter how logical our arguments
or how fervent our appeals,

our words will accomplish nothing
unless God's Spirit prepares the way."

―――

"We can change the course of events
if we go to our knees in believing prayer."

―――

"Prayer is speaking to God --
but sometimes He uses
our times of prayerful silence
to speak to us in return."

―――

"Before prayer changes others,
it first changes us."

―――

"Prayer should be as much a part of our lives as breathing.

Don't ever hesitate to take to God whatever is on your heart.

He already knows it anyway, but He doesn't want you
to bear its pain or celebrate its joy alone."

―――

"Avail yourself of the greatest privilege this side of heaven.

Jesus Christ died to make this communion
and communication with the Father
possible."

* * *

Answers to Prayer
PrayerFoundation ™ 24-Hr. Prayerchain

Mar. 3, 2010 - Answer to Prayer:

Dear *Prayer Warriors,*

I want to thank first our Heavenly Father for His love, because He answers always the prayers lifted up for the salvation of the souls.

I thank also all the *Prayer Warriors* who have prayed for my daughter Valy.

She has come out from her trouble and depression, and last Sunday she goes to Church to worship the Lord. It was two years, she don't come to Church Service. Allelluja! God is good and faithful.

May God bless you all, and give strength and power to your prayers.

Love in Jesus,

-Aldo (Italy)

(From the book: *Answers to Prayer* by S.G. Preston)

4. *One Daily Hour of Prayer*

4.1 7 a.m.: The Book of Psalms

*"Abba Pastor was approached
by a Brother Monk who stated:*

*'Many different temptations are
constantly entering my thoughts.
I fear that my soul is in danger.'*

*The Elder asked the Brother
to go outside with him.*

It was very windy outside.

*Monk Pastor
said to the Brother,*

*'Spread your cloak
and capture the wind
within its folds!*

*The Brother looked
at the older monk
incredulously and said,
'Abba, that's impossible!'*

*You're right, the Elder said,
"No one can catch the wind.*

*If you can't even do that,
how do you think you can
keep tempting thoughts
from entering
your mind?*

You can't!

*Your duty is simply
to not give in
to them.'"*

-Sayings of the Desert Fathers

7 a.m.

D aylight is gradually increasing as I return to the Chapel for my Daily Hour of Prayer. It is now 7 a.m.

Hermiston joins me, laying down at my right. Baklava, Batman, Baby Blue, and Barbaro, are our four monastery cats.

After rubbing up against me as a hint that they would like to be petted, they will lay down on the large red Persian carpet, between myself and the altar.

Pets in the Chapel

Yes, we allow our pets in our Chapel! St. Francis would approve.

One of our cats, Batman, a Tuxedo cat who looks like he is wearing a Batman Cape and Cowl, climbs up into my lap as I sit cross-legged on the floor.

After about 15 minutes, two of the cats have moved, each now sitting on their own Japanese seat pillows.

These are meant for people, but each is just the perfect size to hold a curled up cat, and apparently of just the right softness!

Our cats and our Scottish Terrier almost always join me when I enter our Chapel.

They will usually remain near me for as long as I am praying there.

Prayer in Montana

I have many precious memories of my hour of prayer over the years. Living awhile in the countryside of Montana, I remember often climbing up onto mountains to pray.

There is a distinct crisp, clean smell found only in untouched western forests of pine and fir. Bright, cascading streams, filled with trout, small ponds, and beaver dams, could be found flowing down through every ravine in the mountains.

There to be seen and enjoyed, were spectacular views of the valley far below, the mountains on the farther side of the valley fading gradually into a blue haze in the distance.

S.G. Preston

1970's - Unlocked Doors

In the 1970's, Anglican and Catholic Churches were still always open for prayer. Most Protestant churches were locked. As an Evangelical Protestant, this did not seem right to me.

At that time in rural Montana, in the early 1970's, even many private homes did not lock their doors. Children of Ranchers would tell me that their parents had lost the keys to their house decades before, and could not lock their house even if they had wanted to.

They also told me that they would go on vacation every year for weeks at a time, with their house left unlocked, and think nothing of it.

The Little Church

I was then living out in the countryside of Montana, about five miles away from a little town of 5,000 people. A very small wooden Anglican Church had been built 100 years earlier in the town, and it was always left open for prayer. For many months I went to this little church every morning for my Daily Hour of Prayer.

I can still see in my memory, the morning sunlight streaming through the stained-glass windows. The church faced east, as has been the practice from the earliest centuries of Christianity.

Praying Psalm 22

There was a crucifix over the altar, and for a few weeks I was kneeling there daily; memorizing, meditating on, and praying Psalm 22. This psalm prophetically describes the Crucifixion of Christ.

One Wednesday morning as I was praying, church members began trickling in, followed by the Priest, who officiated at a Service. This was quite surprising to me at the time, but pleasantly so.

After this, I made it a point to schedule my prayer time an hour before the Service every Wednesday.

4.2 Attending Bible College

"Prayer makes a godly man, and puts within him the mind of Christ,
the mind of humility, of self-surrender,
of service, of pity, and of prayer.

If we really pray, we will become more like God,
or else we will quit praying."

-E.M. Bounds (1835 - 1913)
Methodist Pastor

Practicing Flute in Front of an Altar

I attended an Evangelical Bible College belonging to the Christian & Missionary Alliance Denomination. The school campus had been purchased from the Jesuits (The Society of Jesus), having originally been built as one of their schools.

An elective course that I took was flute lessons, my other classes being either Biblical Studies or Christian History. Practice rooms for the musicians were unique; each room contained an elaborate polished marble altar, and each altar was engraved with a different suitable inscription.

Friday Missionary Speakers

The Jesuits had also used these rooms as practice rooms, but for the training of those studying for the priesthood. Part of the purchase from the Jesuits included a very beautiful Chapel, which we students attended daily.

My favorite Chapel service was on Friday, when the guest speaker would always be a missionary, and they could be from anywhere in the world. There might be an Indian national from India, wearing traditional robes, an African in their country's more colorful clothing, or an American of any ethnicity, stationed in Brazil, or Thailand, or France.

Although it was a very long time ago, I still remember that a pilot from the *Mission Aviation Fellowship* spoke one Friday, and someone from *Wycliffe Bible Translators* on another.

M.K. - Missionary Kid

Talking to the Professors and Students was very edifying. Our Professor of the Old Testament referred to himself as a *completed Messianic Jew*.

One of my fellow students was the son of a missionary. He told me that his family had been stationed in Papua New Guinea.

This student, about eighteen years old, said that he remembered being nine years old and watching, from the top of a mountain, a tribe fighting a war in the valley below.

He told me that he had often watched battles between native New Guinean tribes. That the way they fought their wars, as soon as someone was either killed or injured badly, the battle would end.

Praying Five Psalms a Day

Speaking at a Chapel Service, one of the Professors told us how he prayed the Psalms. He said that he had started as a young student himself, and had been praying the Psalms daily for twenty-five years. His practice was to pray five psalms each day, praying all 150 Psalms every month. He said that he always prayed them out loud.

He also said that he had never memorized a single psalm word for word, but that he could tell you what each and every psalm contained, just from memory.

No Kneelers

One day I noticed that in the College Chapel, there were holes in the backs of the pews where kneelers had once been attached, but the actual kneelers had been removed.

Curious, I asked one of my instructors, "What happened to the kneelers?"

He told me that the College had removed them when they bought the building.

"Why?" I asked, shocked. I have used and appreciated kneelers as long as I have been a Christian.

"Well," he said, "we just don't use kneelers in our type of Services."

No Pews

How sad, I thought, looking at the small, forlorn looking holes in the backs of the pews, and wishing the kneelers were still there.

In our own Chapel we do not have kneelers either, for we do not have any pews!

We do kneel often, of course, but our knees rest on the enormous red Persian carpet that covers most of the floor.

4.3 Visiting the Canadian Rockies

*"Have you entered into
the treasures of the snow?"*

-Job 38:22

———

*"To be a Christian without prayer
is no more possible than to be alive
without breathing."*

-Martin Luther (1483-1546)

5 a.m.

In my mid-twenties, three summers in a row, I camped in Banff and Jasper National Parks in Alberta and British Columbia, in Canada. It was always a challenge to wake up an hour before anyone else to pray, for everyone generally arose at sunrise even after a late night of campfire fellowship.

For me, my usual 6 or 7 a.m. prayer time was replaced by 5 a.m.

Since it was British Columbia, about every third day it would be raining, as I left my tent in the dark with a Bible and a sheepskin. The sheepskin came in very handy to place on wet ground or even dry dirt, when I would discover the covering shelter of a tree or a rock outcropping. It provided a way to avoid sharp stones, dirt, and wet vegetation.

Canadian Rockies

One day when it wasn't raining, I went a little farther than usual, climbing the mountainside above the campground, and going off trail directly into the wilderness. Hiking through relatively thick undergrowth, I accidentally stumbled upon what looked like the framework of a Native American longhouse.

It was made of sticks lashed together with rawhide thongs, and was about ten feet high and twenty-five feet long. I suppose it must have been made by some sort of Canadian Boy Scout type of group.

A Natural Chapel

Situated in a small vale, or depression, it overlooked a spectacular view of the entire valley.

A winding Canadian river and parallel highway could be seen descending from the glacier-covered mountains to the campground below.

Placing my sheepskin where the front doorway would once have been, I opened my Bible to the Book of Psalms, and praised God for the wonderful view.

I praised Him also for the truly awesome natural chapel that He had given me to pray in. Each summer for the next two years, I would return to the exact same spot to pray.

Snow

One day I woke up with my tent covered in a quarter inch of snow.

This was in early August! Only a few short hours later it had all melted away.

Several decades later, I returned to Banff and Jasper National Parks with Linda one summer. What led up to it was: I had worked for two and a half years straight without a single day off.

It was the longest period in my entire life that I have ever done this.

Example of the Desert Fathers

To support ourselves, we were both working 24 hours a week at a local Craft Market, two 12-hour days each week.

Linda also had an additional part-time job, to bring her paid working hours to 40 per week.

I was working a third 12 hour day of related business, in order for us to be able to devote ourselves to full-time Christian ministry.

My work on *The PrayerFoundation*™ website and its related ministries of *prayer encouragement* involved four eight to twelve hour days, volunteering without receiving any compensation, during my four days a week *"off"* from the work I did to earn a living.

S.G. Preston

A Labor of Love

I was able to donate a minimum of 40 hours a week to our ministry for twelve years. It was a labor of love for the Lord. I still do this, continuing in ministry, but no longer on the website. We do this so that we can practice our ministry without charge four days of the week, as a gift to God.

In living this way, we feel that we are following the example of the Desert Fathers. They would sell the baskets that they made while they prayed, in order to support themselves, and also to have money to give away in Christian service.

But ever since that time, I have always made certain to take off at least one day a week.

Learning to Ski

The very next year we made up for not having any days off for so long, by taking three days a week off for eight months straight. Linda had always wanted to learn how to ski, so one December we signed up for six hours of ski classes.

Neither of us had ever skied before. We couldn't even stand up on our rented skis, and fell down about every five minutes.

The three to six year-olds we were sharing the beginner's area with, seemed to be doing much better than us, so we thought we would be stuck on the beginner's *"Bunny Slope"* for at least a year, but we were determined not to give up.

Too Old to Learn?

Everyone we knew told us that we were too old to learn how to ski.

But they had also said that we were too old to learn how to ride horses or learn how to sail, and we had done both of those things, so we just ignored them.

We skied three days a week, every single week, from the beginning of December through the end of July. It didn't matter to us how cold the temperature was, or how strong the wind was, or if it was blizzarding, or even the couple of times when it was raining.

99

Skiing With Linda

In fact, twice we arrived at the Ski Resort and it was closed because the weather was too extreme! It took two months before we moved up from the *Bunny Slope* to the *Green*-marked runs, considered *"Easiest."*

We next moved up to the *Blue*-marked runs, considered *"More Difficult,"* and eventually skied the *Black Diamond*-marked runs, considered *"Most Difficult."*

There are also runs marked *Double Black Diamond, "Experts Only,"* but we decided to pass on those. We just wanted to have fun, not become professional Ski Instructors!

All of this skiing was accomplished in only one winter season.

How were we able to progress so fast? We estimated that we had skied in our first season the same amount of time that most people skied in their first ten years of skiing.

Also, when you ski with Linda, every run is a *timed race* to see who finishes first! And if she beats you twice in a row, the first thing she wants to know is: *did she also beat her previous time?*

Each day on the slopes we would ski for six hours straight, with only one half hour break to warm up from the cold and eat a protein bar.

U.S. Olympic Team & X-Gamers

We are blessed to live only an hour and a half away from Mt. Hood, in Oregon. Several ski resorts have summer skiing for part of the summer, but Mt. Hood is the only mountain in North America where you can ski *all* summer.

Because of this, the U.S. Olympic Ski Team trains on Mt. Hood every summer, and so do the X-Games competitors.

The lift lines are only about five minutes long in the winter, but they can be twenty minutes long in the summer, because half of the runs have melted, and because skiers come to ski here from as far away as Canada and Mexico.

The trade-off is, in June and July we could ski wearing shorts and t-shirts! This summer skiing is only possible because it is done on Palmer Glacier, which never melts.

Return to Lake Louise

After two and a half years without a single day off, Linda became very worried about me, and finally felt that *"enough was enough."*

Without telling me until the day before we boarded a plane for Canada, she booked a room at *Chateau Lake Louise* in Banff National Park for us for two nights, beginning on my birthday.

I remembered that, decades before, each year when I had tent camped nearby, I had gone into the Lobby of this beautiful Hotel on Lake Louise to write postcards in the Lobby, never imagining that I would ever in my life be able to afford to actually stay there.

Now we were *"camping"* in a very nice room in the Fairmont-owned *Chateau Lake Louise*.

Black Bears

In a previous year in Banff National Park, I had stopped my car next to the road to view a black bear. It seemed to be eating grass, like a cow, but perhaps it was eating insects in the grass.

My window was rolled down, and suddenly the bear was trying to stick its head into the car! I have never rolled a window up so fast (it was the old crank handle type). I was bumping the bear's face with the glass to make him back out. His nose (and teeth!) were less than a foot from my face.

The bear turned and walked directly into the bushes.

There was no place for such a large creature to enter the solid appearing wall of brush, but it disappeared immediately, making no sound at all, not even stepping on and cracking a twig.

I realized then that you could be in the woods with a black bear standing less than a foot away, and you would never know it.

Up the Mountain

We rode horses around scenic Lake Louise, and on switchbacks up the mountain to a rugged log cabin teahouse, hidden high up on the slopes and deep within the woods.

On the ride, we saw bear claw markings on several trees.

Horseback Riding and Canoeing

Linda's horse apparently smelled a bear, or perhaps there was one standing unseen next to the trail, because suddenly her horse reared up on its hind legs, just like in the old cowboy movies, and took off at a gallop.

Linda thought she was going to be bounced from the saddle at any minute, but she was finally able to get her horse under control, after it got enough distance away from whatever had startled it.

At the farther end of the Lake is the most beautiful, scenic glacier that we have ever seen, and we later canoed across the entire lake, and right up to the glacier.

Lake Louise is the most photographed spot in Canada, and if you are ever blessed by God to go there, you will understand why.

4.4 Watch and Pray

*"The Lord led us gradually
to the sin of prayerlessness
as one of the deepest roots
of the problem.*

*No one could claim
to be free from this.*

*Nothing so reveals
a defective spiritual life
in a minister or a congregation
as a lack of believing
and unceasing prayer.*

*Prayer is the pulse
of the spiritual life."*

-Andrew Murray (1828-1917)
Dutch Reformed Pastor in South Africa
Author: *With Christ in the School of Prayer*

The Woman Who Mocked Christian Teachers

Once, mistakenly and regrettably, I read a book by a supposedly Christian woman who wrote (intending it as mockery) that nearly every Christian teacher taught exactly the same thing:

*"To pray for an hour a day,
and to rise up early in the morning
to do it."*

Solomon and the Idols

I later learned that she didn't even believe in the Trinity!

The book had been obtained from a Christian bookstore. What was a book by such a heretical author even doing there? Unfortunately this reflects the sad state of affairs, ignorance of the Bible, and spiritual shallowness in much of the Christian culture of today.

Watch With Me

It reminded me of Solomon allowing the idols of his many non-believing wives to be placed within the very courtyards of God's Temple. Perhaps there is a reason why *"nearly every"* Christian teacher exhorts believers to rise up early and devote an hour to prayer.

As a young Christian I was led to do the same by the Bible and by Christ's example, even as all of the others also were:

"And He came to the disciples,
and found them asleep,
and said to Peter,

'What? Could you not
watch with me one hour?

Watch and pray,
that you enter not
into temptation.

The spirit is willing,
but the flesh is weak.'"

-Matthew 26:40-41
Mark 14:37-38

4.5 A Morning Hour of Prayer

"And in the morning, rising up a
great while before day, He went out,
and departed into a solitary place,
and there prayed."

-Mark 1:35

Prayer in the Morning

There is no one best specific time at which to begin observing a Daily Hour of Prayer. For those of us who choose to practice this spiritual discipline, the actual time we begin may even vary from day to day, depending upon our individual schedules.

For some, the evening may prove to be the only time that is practical; yet, if possible, the example of our Lord encourages as early a time as possible.

John Bunyan advised:

"He who runs from God in the morning,
will scarcely find Him the rest of the day."

Time Alone With God

I remember many years ago knowing a Christian who never got around to praying until the end of the day; always putting everything else first.

Every evening he would complain:

"Why am I always doing this
at the end of the day?

I need to be having
my prayer time
the first thing in the morning
so I can receive
the benefit of it all day."

Harmony With God

Hudson Taylor put it this way:

> *"Do not have your concert first,*
> *and then tune your instrument*
> *afterwards.*
>
> *Begin the day*
> *with the Word of God and prayer,*
> *and get first of all into harmony*
> *with Him."*

Of course, we already observe several set times of prayer during the day, and turn our thoughts in prayer to God all throughout day, as often as it occurs to us to do so.

But here I am speaking of a special set aside longer period of an entire hour of personal prayer.

A Personal Prayer Tip:

Get Enough Sleep Before Morning Prayer

Something I have learned over the years is that if one desires to pray early in the morning, the single most important thing to insure success is going to sleep early enough the night before.

This is so basic, so obvious, and yet so important, that I think I should repeat it:

> *If one desires to pray early in the morning,*
> *the single most important thing*
> *to insure success*
>
> *is going to sleep early enough*
> *the night before.*

4.6 Change the World School of Prayer

*"Satan will contest
every hour you spend in
Bible reading
or prayer."*

-Billy Graham (1918-2018)

Dick Eastman

In the mid-1970's I had already been praying an hour a day for several years, when I attended an inspiring all-day Seminar held in a local Church.

It was *The Change the World School of Prayer*, which was conceived to be *a prayer encouragement ministry* to set aside an hour daily for prayer, and to pray and meditate on the Psalms.

I was greatly benefitted by taking the course. This fine ministry was founded by, and at that time still taught by, Dick Eastman. He later became President of the *Every Home for Christ* ministry (formerly: *Christian Literature Crusade*).

Linda and I were later blessed to be able to attend together a class taught by Dick Eastman at a Christian Music Festival in the 1990's.

Praying One Hour a Day for the Rest of Their Lives

Included with the teaching Seminar when I attended it, was an instruction booklet and some *cassettes*. Yes, it was that long ago! There was a recording of the Book of Psalms, and a teaching cassette by the Roman Catholic Archbishop Fulton J. Sheen.

When I looked into this same ministry some years later, this recording was no longer being offered. It was a recording of a speech that the Archbishop had often given.

This was the same class that he would teach to newly installed Bishops under his jurisdiction. Archbishop Sheen required all of the new Bishops to commit to *praying one hour a day for the rest of their lives.*

Television

I remember our family watching the then *Bishop* Fulton J. Sheen on television when I was very young, only six to nine years old.

For the purpose of understanding the following story, keep in mind that there were only *one to three* channels on televisions back then, and no way to record a show to watch later!

Only Three Television Channels

We lived between Chicago, which had two television channels, and Milwaukee, which had one, so we were actually able to receive three channels. This was very exceptional in the U.S. at that time, most of which had only one or two channels.

Actually, there was an additional channel on most televisions, the Government's Educational Channel, but I did not know of anyone who ever watched that, so I don't count it.

Bishop Sheen Vs. Milton Berle

Bishop Sheen was an extremely interesting speaker, and his total number of viewers exceeded the television program that had previously been number one in the ratings.

That was the popular comedian Milton Berle, whose television show aired at the exact same time on a different channel. Once, when asked by an interviewer how it was possible that Bishop Sheen had more viewers than he did, Berle quipped:

"He has better writers."

S.G. Preston

Answers to Prayer
PrayerFoundation ™ 24-Hr. Prayerchain

Aug. 18, 2007 - Prayer Request

Our Seminary in Russia, *****, will have a visit from the Sanitation Department. The visit will be led by *****, who just last week began a conversation with our Provost *****, with the following words:

"I remember you. I still don't like you (from the last visit)...
Why are you poisoning our young people? You are not Russian Orthodox!"

Although ***** did his best to disarm the situation, it still set the tone for the remainder of the conversation.

***** negotiated further with her. She agreed to visit the Seminary for an inspection. As it turns out, she has enough clout in her department to say either:

"I close your building down" or: "I will certify your building."

So we at *****, request for your prayers. Please pray for this Inspector. May God turn her heart toward us, so that she will not do something against us, but rather do all the paper work the way we need for the licensing process.

Thank you very much in advance, for your prayers.

*****, President
***** Seminary

Answer to Prayer - Aug. 22, 2007 (Four days later.)

We have some great news from Moscow! Today, ***** from the Sanitary Department, came to inspect the Seminary.

As ***** came to the school, ***** welcomed her at the door, and noticed a change in her demeanor. Today she was friendly and very accommodating.

Obviously, she had a change of attitude about the Seminary, and approached today's business with an open mind.

She toured various sections of the Seminary, and pointed out only one minor issue that needed to be corrected: too many computers in the lab.

The classrooms, offices, and the library were all approved without a problem -- thus all of the rooms used for *educational purposes* are now certified. We are now breathing a big sigh of relief.

Thank you for your prayers on our behalf!

And perhaps the biggest answer to prayer? Because ***** was late for her next appointment, she asked ***** to drive back to her office (she had taken public transportation to the school).

***** gladly complied, and an interesting and engaging conversation took place in the car, that eventually focused on the faith.

A friend of hers had converted to the Adventist movement and ***** had several questions. ***** took advantage of the moment, and shared with her about his faith.

As ***** told me:

"We talked about Christ Jesus, about the way of Salvation, about His Death and Resurrection, and about common things between Russian Orthodoxy and Evangelicals (i.e., His Resurrected Life and 2nd Coming).

Wonderful, just wonderful! Glory to God! Hallelujah! Praise Him!"

Last week, she was antagonistic against Evangelicals. Today, she was openly engaged in a conversation about the faith. Such a change in her disposition can only have come through the Holy Spirit!

Thank you for your prayers.

Sincerely,

*****, President
***** Seminary

(From the book: *Answers to Prayer* by S.G. Preston)

5. *Abiding in Christ*

5.1 Monk Telemachus Ends the Colosseum Games

"We shall see how the Scriptures condemn the amphitheater.

If we can maintain that it is right to indulge in the cruel, the impious, and the fierce, then let us go there."

-Tertullian (Writing c. 210 A.D.)
From: *The Shows or De Spectaculis*
(*The Spectacles*); Chapter 19

———

"...some of them (the Gnostics) do not even keep away from that bloody spectacle hateful to both God and men, in which gladiators either fight with wild beasts or individually encounter one another."

-Irenaeus of Lyon (Writing 183-186 A.D.)
From: *Against Heresies*; 1:6:3

One Person Can Make A Difference

When we abide in Christ; Christ also living in us and through us; our influence on the people and world around us becomes, as David Brainerd prayed:

"...utterly disproportionate to who we are."

St. Telemachus' birth date is unknown. The last known gladiator fight in Rome was on January 1, 404 A.D., so this is usually given as the date of St. Telemachus' martyrdom (he is also known as: St. Almachus).

I first heard this story on a Christian Radio station. Having missed the beginning of the program, I do not know who was speaking, but the story was told beautifully.

National Prayer Breakfast

The story of *Telemachus* and how the holding of the Colosseum Games and Gladiatorial Contests came to an end, has often been repeated.

Even American President Ronald Reagan told the story of *"the little monk"* at the Annual National Prayer Breakfast on February 2, 1984. He liked it so much, that he told the story again the next year at the National Prayer Breakfast held on January 31, 1985.

Unfortunately, there are some mistakes in the story that are usually perpetuated, whenever it is given. Here is a brief summary of the story as you will often hear it:

In the fourth century a little monk named Telemachus from Asia (modern day Turkey comprises the Roman province of Asia; what we today call Asia Minor), was led by an inner voice to go to Rome without knowing why. He followed the crowds to the Colosseum. Two gladiators were fighting, and Telemachus tried to get between them to stop them, shouting three times:

"In the name of Christ, forbear!"

Telemachus was killed by being run through with the sword of one of the gladiators. When the crowd saw the little monk lying dead in a pool of blood, they fell silent, leaving the stadium, one by one.

Because of Telemachus' death, three days later, the Emperor by decree ended the Games.

Errors in the Story

There are two major errors found in this account:

(1.) That the event described above occurred in the fourth century. It actually occurred in the early 400's A.D., which is the *fifth* century.

(2.) That Telemachus was killed by a gladiator's sword, the crowd then leaving one by one, until all had left the Colosseum.

In fact, Telemachus was killed through being stoned to death by the furious crowd, enraged that someone would dare to interfere with their *"entertainment."*

What Actually Happened

Some critics claim that Telemachus' death cannot have ended the Colosseum Games, because the Games were held until the early fifth century. This a false argument, because these critics have accepted the wrong dating of the event.

They are correct about the dating of the ending of the Games, but wrong in contending that Telemachus' death was not the event that caused it.

The true story is found in the writings of Theodoret, Bishop of Cyrrhus (or: Cyrus) in Syria (393-457 A.D.). Theodoret's *Ecclesiastical History* covers the period of time up until 429 A.D. (the early fifth century). I quote it here:

Honorius the Emperor & Telemachus the Monk

"Honorius, who inherited the empire of Europe, put a stop to the gladiatorial combats which had long been held at Rome. The occasion of his doing so arose from the following circumstance.

A certain man of the name of Telemachus had embraced the ascetic life. He had set out from the East and for this reason had repaired to Rome.

There, when the abominable spectacle was being exhibited, he went himself into the stadium, and stepping down into the arena, endeavoured to stop the men who were wielding their weapons against one another.

The spectators of the slaughter were indignant, and inspired by the triad fury of the demon who delights in those bloody deeds, stoned the peacemaker to death.

When the admirable Emperor was informed of this, he numbered Telemachus in the number of victorious martyrs, and put an end to that impious spectacle."

-Theodoret, Bishop of Cyrus; *The Ecclesiastical History*
(*Of Honorius the Emperor and Telemachus the Monk*)
Book 5, Chapter 26

5.2 But One Thing is Needful

*"Mary has chosen
that good part,
which shall not be
taken away
from her."*

-Luke 10:42

A Daily Hour of Power

A rchbishop Fulton J. Sheen, on a teaching tape, said that in over forty years, he had never missed a single day of his daily hour of prayer: with one possible exception.

I may have forgotten some of the details of the story, but here is the substance of it:

Attending a one-day conference in Europe, the Archbishop had been traveling on a very tight schedule.

Arriving on an overnight *"redeye"* flight into the city in which he was to speak that morning, he hadn't slept very well on the plane, and was exhausted.

A driver had picked him up at the airport, taking him directly to the conference, where he was to be the first speaker.

Later that day, as soon as the last speaker addressed the conference, the driver was to take the Archbishop immediately back to the airport for his departing flight.

A Daily Hour of Power

There was one open hour and a half time slot between speakers, set aside for lunch.

It offered Archbishop Sheen the only possible time to observe his daily hour of prayer.

He had his driver take him to the nearest Catholic Church and wait outside for him.

God Gives His Beloved Sleep (Psalm 127:2)

The Archbishop entered the church, kneeled down on one of the pew kneelers, and was so tired that he immediately fell asleep.

Upon awaking, he looked at his watch, and discovered that he had slept for exactly one hour.

As the driver returned him to the conference, Archbishop Sheen wondered if he had "kept his prayer time" or not?

Had God let him sleep during his daily hour of prayer, because God knew how badly he needed the rest, or had he simply *"missed"* his prayer time; the only one in what would turn out to be over forty years of faithful observance?

The Archbishop said that he had never been quite certain either way.

5.3 Spiritual Disciplines Not Ends in Themselves

"A monk asked one of the Abbas a question,

'There were two monks:
one stayed always in his Hermitage.
This monk often fasted for six days in a row.
He also observed many other spiritual practices.

The other Brother spent all of his time
caring for those who were ill.

Which of the two monks' actions
was God more pleased with?'

The Elder answered,
'If the Monk that fasted six days in a row,
had in addition hung himself from a hook
by his nose,

that Brother's actions would still not equal
that of the monk who cared for those
who were ill.'"

-Sayings of the Desert Fathers

Following Christ's Example

It has been wisely said that one is always a beginner in prayer, no matter how many decades they have been praying.

However, keeping this in mind as a spiritual truism, it is also our cherished hope to learn, experience, and by the grace of God, progress somehow in this most important area of our walk with God.

E.M. Bounds encourages us in this by saying:

"We can never expect to grow in the likeness of our Lord
unless we follow His example and give more time
to communion with the Father.

A revival of real praying would produce
a spiritual revolution."

Spiritual Disciplines

The spiritual disciplines are certainly not to be viewed as ends in themselves.

If we are reading the Bible, praying and fasting to become *"more spiritual,"* and when interrupted, react in anger or impatience to our spouse or children, we have obviously missed the point.

We are no longer, moment by moment:

> *"...walking in the Spirit..."*
>
> -Galatians 5:16

Time Alone With God

E.M. Bounds also admonishes us to remember that; although he believes we *do* need to spend much time in prayer with God, in order to grow in this area and become a man or woman of prayer; God is interested in the *quality* of that time, not in its mere quantity.

Rev. Bounds taught:

> *"We would not have any think*
> *that the value of their prayers*
> *is to be measured by the clock,*
>
> *but our purpose is to impress*
> *on our minds*
> *the necessity of being*
> *much alone with God;*
>
> *and that if this feature has not been*
> *produced by our faith,*
> *then our faith is of a feeble*
> *and surface type."*

5.4 Abiding in Christ is Our Goal

*"The most valuable thing the Psalms do for me
is to express the same delight in God
which made David dance."*

-C.S. Lewis (1898-1963)
Author: *Mere Christianity*
and *The Chronicles of Narnia*

True Prayer

Being in communion with God, maintaining our relationship with and abiding in Him, *is* an end in itself.

There can be no true prayer without real communion with God.

That is what prayer *is*, after all: having a relationship with God.

I quote here a selection of Scriptures that we have used in worship. We do not include the verse references in our responses.

These verses express the real, authentic, *lived* Christianity that is the goal and calling of our ministry:

Officiant: *"Jesus said:*

All: *'I am the vine, you are the branches. Those who abide in Me, and I in them, bring forth much fruit; for without Me you can do nothing."* (John 15:5)

"Those who say that they abide in Him ought also to walk, even as He walked..." (1 John 2:6)

"If you abide in Me, and My words abide in you, you shall ask what you will, and it shall be done for you." (John 15:7)

"Walk in the Spirit, and you shall not fulfill the desires of the flesh." (Galatians 5:16)

Officiant: *"He who has called you is holy, so you should also be holy in everything you do."* (1 Peter 1:15)

All: *"For in Him we live, and move, and have our being."* (Acts 17:28)

S.G. Preston

The Psalms Speak *For* Us

Remember how George Müller said that the first thing upon awaking, he would go to prayer, and sometimes couldn't seem to get *"...in the Spirit..."*?

Then he discovered that he should first read the Word of God until he was led to pray.

It is often my practice, upon arising, to pray Psalm 5, following the example of Athanasius of Alexandria.

In the Psalms, the Word of God and prayer are already combined; so, I too, although unwittingly, have managed to avoid that problem!

Later in this book, we will look in depth at what Athanasius has to say concerning the Psalms in his *Letter to Marcellinus*. He will instruct us that (Boldface mine):

> *"...the Psalms have a*
> *unique place in the Bible*
>
> *because most of the Scripture*
> *speaks **to** us,*
>
> *while the Psalms*
> *speak **for** us."*

5.5 God Himself Will Teach You How to Pray

"(The Psalms are) a little Bible,
wherein everything
contained in the entire Bible
is beautifully and briefly
comprehended."

-Martin Luther (1483-1546)

Deciding to Pray

We will now look at ways of praying for a complete hour, set aside daily. One can simply decide to do it, as I did when I was still a new Christian. In the beginning it will often be one of the hardest things you have ever done.

An hour may sometimes seem like it is lasting for days. How can you think of enough to say, to pray for, to be able to fill up an entire hour? You have prayed for seemingly *two* hours, but when you look at the clock, a mere five minutes has passed!

God Gives His Beloved Sleep...Again

Sometimes I would get out of bed to pray my Daily Hour of Prayer at 3 a.m., and twice upon doing so, I realized that I must have dozed off, because my head suddenly jerked up. This does, however, make the hour go by much more quickly!

Just *keep praying every day* and you will at some point realize that you have learned how to pray.

Everyone Prays Differently

Another way is to divide the hour up into various types of prayer. We talked earlier about nine of them:

Supplication, Intercession, Praise,
Thanksgiving, Adoration, Silence,
Confession, Scripture Memorization,
Meditation On God's Word.

Dick Eastman's Book:

The Hour That Changes the World

...has a pie chart that does this, covering many different types of prayer. However, you will find that at times, you will still run out of words, have gone through all of the entire hour's-worth of types of prayer in the first ten minutes, and still have the same problem.

The fact is that everyone prays differently. Historically, spiritual advisors in monasteries do not like to give too specific advice for this reason.

Prayer Practices

Perhaps as a new Christian my *"learn to swim by jumping in the water"* approach was all right – *one size fits all.* However, I myself actually learned how to swim by taking lessons as a child at the YMCA.

This is why our website has so many different types of prayer practices posted on it. We have tried all of them as we were studying them. Some we practice for a time, and then may go back to, years later. *But no one could possibly observe all of them, all of the time.*

Error of Stoicism...Again

Let us recall once again, what C.S. Lewis, quoting Blaise Pascal, said about the *Error of Stoicism*:

> *"Thinking that we*
> *can do always,*
> *what we can do*
> *sometimes."*

Still, one or more of them may be right for, and greatly helpful to one person, while others may be helpful to another. And different prayer practices may be helpful to yourself, or someone else, at different times in life.

I have found, for myself, praying the Psalms to be a very beautiful experience and spiritually rewarding.

Martin Luther and the Psalms

Let God Himself teach you how to pray, through His Word. Remember Mary and Martha? Have a seat at Christ's feet, in His presence.

There is an entire section of the Bible that God has provided for just this purpose. It is the Book of Psalms, and it is not only *instructional* learning, it is also *hands on* learning.

Martin Luther taught:

"For everyone,
on every occasion,
can find in the Psalms
that which fits their needs,
which they feel
to be appropriate,

as if they had been set there
just for their sake..."

5.6 Learning to Sail, Learning to Pray

"And immediately Jesus made
the Disciples get into the boat
and go before Him to the other side,
while He sent the multitudes away.

After he had sent them away,
He went up onto a mountain
by Himself to pray;
and when night fell,
He was there alone.

But the boat was now far out
in the midst of the sea,
tossing in the waves,
for the wind was
against them.

And sometime
between 3 a.m. and 6 a.m.,
Jesus went out to them
walking on the sea."

-Matthew 14:22-24

Getting Out On the Water

Instructional learning always needs to be accompanied by *hands on* learning. This is why after Medical School, Doctors learn by *doing*, in *residency*, before their education is considered to be complete.

Peter could see Jesus walk on the water, but he needed to do it himself. Of course, he still needed some help from the Lord!

When Linda and I were learning how to sail, I discovered the same principles to be true. First, we both completed the Beginning and Advanced levels of the Coast Guard Safety Training classes for operating boats.

Next, I took both the Beginning and Intermediate Course levels of *"on the water"* sailing instruction. Our instructor gave each of us a *"safety, theory, and basics"* instruction manual to read:

"Memorize it," he told us,
*"but remember that
you can't learn how to sail
from a book...*

*you have to actually
get out on the water
in a sailboat!"*

From Oregon to the Florida Keys

We purchased a 22-foot sailboat with a towing trailer. Without ever having sailed it in Portland, we took off cross-country to Key West, Florida, to sail it in the Gulf of Mexico and on the Atlantic Ocean.

Key West is located on the southernmost tip of the Florida Keys, only 90 miles from Cuba.

We would later trailer the boat up to the San Juan Islands, between Seattle and Canada.

There, among many other enjoyable experiences, we had two porpoises surf in the wake of our bow waves. Interestingly, in the San Juan Islands, porpoises are black and white, like miniature Orcas.

Later we did see an entire pod of Orcas, also known as Killer Whales, and even watched a mother and baby Orca dive under our boat, coming up on the other side.

Traveling across the country, we used the sailboat as our place to sleep.

Among the Redwoods

Our first stops were at Redwood National Park in northern California, and the O.K. Corral in Tombstone, Arizona; the place where Wyatt Earp and his brothers had their famous shootout with the Clanton Gang.

When we pulled up outside the Corral, two women ran out to us, joking:

*"Look! The sailboat we ordered
has finally arrived!"*

124

At the Grand Canyon

It was January. Parked on the South Rim of the Grand Canyon, we awoke to find a quarter inch of snow on our boat. We quickly discovered that we would not be able to leave the Grand Canyon until the snow melted.

Our sailboat and trailer could not be towed up the slick, snow-covered slopes. The wheels just spun uselessly, with the entire trailer and boat sliding sideways off the road.

Blessedly, the snow was all melted by 1 p.m. that afternoon, and we were able to continue our journey.

Carlsbad Caverns

Traveling through the seemingly endless barren red desert of New Mexico, we were stopped in the middle of nowhere by a border patrol immigration officer who asked us:

"Where are you going?"

"Carlsbad Caverns," we answered.

Once more he looked our sailboat over suspiciously (was it full of undocumented workers being smuggled into New Mexico?).

As if he was not certain whether we knew something that he was not aware of, he paused, and then informed us, almost as if he were asking a question:

"Ain't no water up there...?"

The Alamo and New Orleans

Our next stops included the Alamo and nearby Riverwalk in San Antonio, Texas. Then we traveled into Louisiana to visit Bourbon Street and the French Quarter in New Orleans.

On our return trip, we were surprised to find that it was now *Mardi Gras*. This was like visiting two totally different cities!

It was a very nice experience to have our Morning Prayer in a different part of the country each day.

A J.I. Packer Prayer Tip:

Meditating (Thinking Deeply) On Scripture Leads to Prayer, Praise, and Knowledge of God

> *"How can we turn our knowledge about God*
> *into knowledge of God?*
> *The rule for doing this is simple but demanding.*
> *It is that we turn each Truth that we learn about God*
> *into meditation before God,*
> *leading to prayer and praise to God."*

-J.I. Packer (1926-2020)
Author: *Knowing God*

A Lay Monk Bob Prayer Tip:

Pray 5 Min. the First Day, & Add 5 Min. Each Day After

Lay Monk Bob told me once, that he had set a timer for five minutes, and then increased it by an additional five minutes every day, until he was praying an hour.

A Personal Prayer Tip:

Praying by Memorizing a Psalm

Set aside an hour per day, or begin first with half an hour per week, or whatever amount of time you may choose.

Pray for current needs. This will take you about five minutes, some days perhaps as much as ten. Take as long as you like.

Next choose a favorite psalm and begin memorizing the first verse. Most Christians' favorite psalm will be the 23rd Psalm, but yours may be different.

Slowly, meditatively -- probably over a period of weeks -- it does not really matter if you ever finish memorizing this psalm. You will, though!

God is speaking to you through his Word, and you are praying to Him in a biblical way used by all of the great saints in the Bible, both in the Old Testament and in the New Testament.

1. Praying Memorized Scripture

If you are allowing an hour a day, you will partially know one or two verses by the end of the first hour. By the next day you may have already forgotten them. Start over. It will be easier this time and you will even get a little farther along.

Memorizing is often: *"Two steps forward, one step back."* Eventually you will have an entire psalm memorized and you can now pray it without needing to read it.

Our Lord Jesus Himself, as well as James, Peter, John, and the other Disciples, probably all began learning how to do this when they were about three years old. Perhaps it's about time you learned how to do it, too!

2. Spontaneous Prayer

Sorry, you're praying *too fast*. You didn't even hear the words. This is why many contemporary Christians *only* pray extemporaneously. *You should pray spontaneously also, it is not an either/or situation.* Although, as you have probably noticed, there are many Christians whose *spontaneous* prayers often fall into exactly the same repetitive phrases.

3. My Meditation All Day Long

Slow down so that you're hearing the words...about the same speed as if you were *reading* them out loud. Your mind is now engaged on God's Word as if you were reading it. Much better! Slow down another gear into *meditative* mode; thinking deeply on the Word of God, savoring it.

The words of the Psalm have now lowered from your head to your heart, and you can feel them there. We want to *"hide the Word"* there, *"in our hearts"* (Psalm 119:11). This will help later in standing against sin. Right now, it will aid us in entering into God's presence and sitting at Christ's feet, where we can say with the Psalmist:

"O how I love Your law! It is my meditation all day long."

-Psalm 119:97

Canticle of Brother Sun

Originally called *The Canticle of the Creatures*
A song written by St. Francis of Assisi
(1181/1182-1226 A.D.)

Most High, all-powerful,
all-good Lord,
All praise is Yours, all glory,
honor and blessings.

To You alone, Most high,
do they belong;
no mortal lips are worthy
to pronounce Your name.

We praise You, Lord,
for all Your creatures,
especially for Brother Sun,
who is the day through whom
You give us light.

And he is beautiful and radiant
with great splendor;
of You Most High,
he bears Your likeness.

We praise You, Lord,
for Sister Moon and the stars,
in the heavens you have
made them bright,
precious and fair.

We praise You, Lord,
for Brothers Wind and Air,
fair and stormy,
all weather's moods,
by which You cherish all
that you have made.

We praise You, Lord,
for Sister Water,
so useful, humble,
precious and pure.

We praise You, Lord,
for Brother Fire,
through whom
You light the night.
He is beautiful, playful,
robust and strong.

We praise You, Lord,
for Sister Earth,
who sustains us
with her fruits,
colored flowers,
and herbs.

We praise You, Lord,
for those who pardon,
for love of You bear
sickness and trial.

Blessed are those
who endure in peace,
by You Most high,
they will be crowned.

We praise and
bless You, Lord,
and give You thanks,
and serve You
in all humility.

* * *

Answers to Prayer
PrayerFoundation ™ 24-Hr. Prayerchain

Nov. 17, 2001 - Answer to Prayer:

I just wanted to say thank you so much for praying for Dayna and Heather, the two American Christian aid workers in Afghanistan.

Praise God for their freedom! I know Dayna personally and both girls are good friends of my friends. It's really so amazing...

God is so faithful! :)

-Allison (Texas)

Author's Note: Heather and Dayna were held prisoner by the Taliban in Afghanistan.

We had placed them on our *24 -Hr. Prayerchain* for four weeks, at which time the prayers of our thousands of volunteer *Prayer Warriors* in 47 Countries, along with the prayers of other Christians from all over the world were answered, and they were released.

(From the book: *Answers to Prayer* by S.G. Preston)

6. *How to Pray the Psalms*

6.1 Dietrich Bonhoeffer & Praying the Psalms

*"Wherever the Psalter is abandoned,
an incomparable treasure
vanishes from the Christian Church.*

*With its recovery will come
unsuspected power."*

-Dietrich Bonhoeffer (1906-1945)
Author: *The Cost of Discipleship* and
Psalms: The Prayer Book of the Bible

Easier to Pray a Memorized Psalm

Time passes, and as you gradually memorize more and more psalms, you will eventually be able to pray psalms for the entire hour, or longer, without needing to do any more additional memorizing at all.

Or you may decide that you still want to continue with your praying/meditation/memorizing.

You can also *"mix and match."* By doing this, the Lord may guide you into a different way of spending your personal prayer time. At that point just ask the Lord what He would have you do (Acts 9:6). That is what it is all about, anyway!

An Email About Praying the *Psalms*

*"I am having trouble
getting a feeling for the difference
between praying the Psalms,
as opposed to just reading them;*

*especially on the occasions
when the Psalm doesn't seem
to apply to my life
at the time.*

131

Can you explain to me
what the difference is or should be;
in my head or in my heart?

How do I feel
that I am praying them?"

My Reply:

Usually when a verse is especially applicable to something happening in your life -- often some sort of problem -- is when you will feel that you are really praying it.

However, Dietrich Bonhoeffer had a different view of this. He wrote:

"Not what we want to pray is important,
but what God wants us to pray."

This quote is an excerpt from a Prayer Tip of Bonhoeffer's, that we will be looking at again later on, in its full context.

Praise, thanksgiving, and repentance, along with asking for forgiveness are always applicable. Praying very slowly a psalm or psalms that you have memorized, will give you the feel for it.

Most Christians will begin with the 23rd Psalm, the most beautiful of all the psalms. Some may begin with the shortest psalm, Psalm 117, only two verses long.

Three Personal Prayer Tips:

It is Easier to Pray a Psalm You Have Memorized
Pray Scripture, Pray Psalms
Practice Daily Consistent Prayer

It is often much easier for Evangelical Protestants to pray a Psalm that they have memorized.

Those of us who have not come from a Protestant Denomination where written prayers are used in Church; as in Anglican, Lutheran, and Presbyterian Churches; have almost a *"mental block"* about tending to reject written prayers as *"not really praying."*

It can be very difficult for us in the beginning.

Rejecting Scripture?

This puts us in the very odd position of rejecting prayers consisting of Holy Scripture and given to us by God specifically for the purpose of praying them, as being *"no good, not really praying,"* while at the same time thinking that only something we make up out of our heads spontaneously is *"real praying."*

They're *both "real praying,"* of course!

We can do both. Praying extemporaneously is necessary and scriptural. Praying from the Book of Psalms is praying Scripture, prayers God recorded in His inspired Word, specifically for our use as prayers.

The Psalms are truly wonderful to pray, especially when you have them memorized.

Three Dietrich Bonhoeffer Prayer Tips:

Understand How Psalms & Other Bible Prayers Reveal Christ
What Does the Bible Teach Us That God Wants Us to Pray
The Blessing of Morning Prayer

Dietrich Bonhoeffer, in his small book, *Psalms: The Prayer Book of the Bible* writes:

*"Now there is in the Holy Scriptures
a book which is distinguished
from all other books of the Bible by the
fact that it contains only prayers.*

The book is the Psalms.

*It is at first very surprising that there
is a prayerbook in the Bible...*

*If we want to read and to pray
the prayers of the Bible,
and especially the Psalms, therefore,
we must not ask first
what they have to do with us,
but what they have to do
with Jesus Christ.*

*We must ask how we can understand
the Psalms as God's Word,
and then we shall be
able to pray them.*

*It does not depend, therefore,
on whether the Psalms express adequately
that which we feel at a given moment
in our heart...*

*If we are to pray aright,
perhaps it is quite necessary
that we pray contrary
to our entire heart.*

*Not what we want to pray is important,
but what God wants us to pray.*

*If we were dependent entirely on ourselves,
we would probably pray only the fourth petition
of the Lord's Prayer.*

But God wants it otherwise.

*The richness of the Word of God
ought to determine our prayer,
not the poverty
of our heart."*

Dietrich Bonhoeffer On Morning Prayer:

*"The entire day receives order and discipline
when it acquires unity.*

*This unity must be sought and found
in morning prayer.*

It is confirmed in work.

The morning prayer determines the day...

*Temptations which accompany the working day
will be conquered on the basis
of the morning breakthrough
to God.*

S.G. Preston

Squandered time of which we are ashamed,
temptations to which we succumb,
weaknesses and lack of courage in work,

disorganization and lack of discipline in our thoughts
and in our conversation with other men,
all have their origin most often in the neglect
of morning prayer...

The powers to work take hold, therefore,
at the place where we
have prayed to God.

He wants to give us today
the power which we need
for our work."

6.2 Athanasius & Praying the Psalms

"Dead men cannot take effective action;
their power of influence on others lasts only until the grave.

Deeds and actions that energize others belong only to the living."

-St. Athanasius of Alexandria
(Writing c. 293-273 A.D.)
From: *On the Incarnation*

Athanasius: On the Incarnation

St. *Vladimir's Seminary Press* (an Eastern Orthodox Seminary) has a wonderful edition of St. Athanasius' book:

On the Incarnation
With an Introduction by C.S. Lewis.

The Appendix consists of the twenty-two and a half page letter of Athanasius to Marcellinus (probably a monk in Alexandria) on the interpretation of the Psalms.

I recommend reading Athanasius' letter in its entirety. You can also find it posted in several places on the Internet.

Athanasius On Praying the Psalms

Here is a brief excerpt of it (Boldface mine):

"My dear Marcellinus,

> *I once talked with a certain studious old man, who had*
> *bestowed much labor on the Psalter, and discoursed*
> *to me about it with great persuasiveness and charm...*
> *holding a copy of it in his hand the while he spoke.*
> *So I am going to write down for you the things he said.*

...*to those who really study it the Psalter yields special treasure.*

Within it are represented and portrayed in all their great variety
the movements of the human soul.

It is like a picture, in which you see yourself portrayed *and seeing,*
may understand and consequently form yourself
upon the pattern given.

Prohibitions of evildoing are plentiful in Scripture,
but only the Psalter tells you how to obey these orders
and refrain from sin.

But the marvel with the Psalter is that,
barring those prophecies about the Savior
and some about the Gentiles,
the reader takes all its words upon his lips
as though they were his own, *written for his special benefit,*
and takes them and recites them,

not as though someone else were speaking or another person's
feelings being described, but as himself speaking of himself,
offering the words of God as his own heart's utterance,
just as though he himself had made them up.

It is possible for us, therefore to find in the Psalter
not only the reflection of our own soul's state,
together with precept and example for all possible conditions,
*but **also a fit form of words wherewith to please the Lord***
on each of life's occasions,
words both of repentance and of thankfulness,
so that we fall not into sin..."

Advice On Which Psalms to Pray and When

"When you would give thanks to God
*at your affliction's end, sing **Psalm 4**...*

When you see the wicked wanting to ensnare you
and you wish your prayer to reach God's ears
*then wake up early and sing **Psalm 5**.*

For victory over the enemy...
knowing that it is the Son of God
who has thus brought things to a happy issue,
*say to Him **Psalm 9**...*

*If you want to know how Moses prayed, you have **the 90th Psalm**.*

*When you have been delivered from these enemies and oppressors,
then sing **Psalm 18**;*

*and when you marvel at the order of creation...**Psalm 19**...*

*while **Psalm 20** will give you words
to comfort and to pray with others in distress.*

*When you yourself are fed and guided by the Lord
and, seeing it, rejoice, **the 23rd Psalm** awaits you.*

*Do enemies surround you?
Then lift up your heart to God and say **Psalm 25**,
and you will surely see the sinners put to rout.*

*And when you want the right way of approach to God in thankfulness,
with spiritual understanding, sing **Psalm 29**.*

*So then, my son, let whoever reads this book of Psalms
take the things in it quite simply as God-inspired.*

*In every case the words you want are written down for you,
and you can say them as your own."*

Note: see *On the Incarnation: The Treatise De Incarnatione Verbi* by St. Athanasius; With an Introduction by C.S. Lewis. Excerpts quoted from the Appendix: *The Letter of St. Athanasius to Marcellinus On the Interpretation of the Psalms*; p.97-119.

Praying Psalms Without Memorizing

It is a wonderful blessing to have even one psalm memorized. Since you will probably not memorize all 150 of them, you will also want to pray psalms that you have not memorized.

As I have said earlier, I had a Professor in Bible College who had never memorized even *one* psalm, but had prayed five of them daily for twenty-five years; all 150 through each month.

His was a consistency, *a faithfulness* in prayer; day in and day out, year after year, decade after decade. He considered this practice to be of the greatest benefit to him in his Christian life.

138

Praying 5 Psalms a Day

The Psalms are primarily Praise and Prayers (containing many prophecies about Christ). They were written in poetic form originally as Songs for use in the Worship of the Temple.

The traditional Hebrew title is *tehillim* ("praises"), although many of the Psalms are *tephillot* ("prayers").

Half of the *Book of Psalms* was composed by David, inspired by the Holy Spirit: 73-75 Psalms.

It is a great joy to pray 5 Psalms every day.

On a particular date each month you pray the same 5 Psalms – it's like meeting 5 old friends once each month: a different 5 every day!

God will specifically speak to you through one or more verses each day, brought to your special attention by the Holy Spirit.

You are joining in praying the same 5 Psalms each day that other Christians throughout the world are also praying on the same day.

Millions?...tens of millions?...out of a total 2.5 billion Christians worldwide. Know that Christians have done so together in unison for hundreds (or has it been...thousands?) of years.

Many Psalms only take about 3 minutes to pray.

And if you're not a *"reader,"* you can pray along listening to an AudioBible!

If This Seems Like Too Much

Another Option: You can Read (or listen to) One Chapter of the New Testament and Pray One Psalm every day.

The New Testament contains 260 Chapters, so you will read all the way through it every 9 months.

There are 150 Psalms, so you will Pray them all every 5 months.

You will be in God's Word more than many Christians!

Do you think doing this will this change your life?

Yes, I think it will, too!

Daily Chart for Praying 5 Psalms a Day
All 150 Each Month

1st / Psalms 1-5
2nd / Psalms 6-10
3rd / Psalms 11-15
4th / Psalms 16-20
5th / Psalms 21-25
6th / Psalms 26-30
7th / Psalms 31-35
8th / Psalms 36-40
9th / Psalms 41-45
10th / Psalms 46-50
11th / Psalms 51-55
12th / Psalms 56-60
13th / Psalms 61-65
14th / Psalms 66-70
15th / Psalms 71-75
16th / Psalms 76-80
17th / Psalms 81-85
18th / Psalms 86-90
19th / Psalms 91-95
20th / Psalms 96-100
21st / Psalms 101-105
22th / Psalms 106-110
23rd / Psalms 111-118
24th / Psalm 119
25th / Psalms 120-125
26th / Psalms 126-130
27th / Psalms 131-135
28th / Psalms 136-140
29th / Psalms 141-145
30th / Psalms 146-150

Once a year, on Feb. 27th & 28th,
pray 10 Psalms each day.

The 31st of some months
is always a *"Free Day."*

6.3 Spending Much Time in Prayer

*"A Brother came to Abba Theodore
and began to converse with him
about things that he had
not yet put into practice.*

*The old monk said to him,
'You have not found a ship,
or loaded cargo aboard it.*

*Yet, before you have
even begun to sail,
you have already arrived
at the city.*

Do the work first.

*Then you will actually have
the speed that you are making now.'"*

-Sayings of the Desert Fathers

Billy Graham's Prayer Tip:

Be Constant in Prayer

*"Am fear nach gleidh na h-airm san t-sith,
cha bhi iad aige 'n am a' chogaidh."*

*"He that keeps not his arms in time of peace,
will have none in time of war."*

-Old Gaelic Saying.

The call to constancy in prayer is affirmed by many great men and women of prayer. One of these was William Edward Biederwolf, a Presbyterian evangelist in the 1890's who wrote:

*"He who does not pray
when the sun shines,
knows not how to pray
when the clouds arise."*

141

Billy Graham confirmed this truth, which is one of the central messages in all of my books:

> *"True prayer is a way of life,*
> *not just for use in cases of emergency.*
>
> *Make it a habit, and when the need arises*
> *you will be in practice."*

Three O. Hallesby Prayer Tips:

Your Helplessness Aids Your Prayer
Be Still and Enjoy God's Presence
Prayer and Its Answers Define Your Life

O. Hallesby was a Lutheran pastor in Norway who was interred for two years in a Nazi Concentration Camp; he was released when the war ended. He wrote an excellent book on prayer, simply called: *Prayer.*

I cannot recommend this book too much. It has a five-star rating on *Amazon*. Read the posted reviews: they say it all. Ole Hallesby wrote:

> *"Helplessness is your best prayer.*
>
> *It calls from your heart to the heart of God*
> *with greater effect than all your uttered pleas."*

———

> *"Prayer is a fine, delicate instrument.*
> *To use it right is a great art,*
> *a holy art.*
>
> *There is perhaps no greater art*
> *than the art of prayer."*

———

> *"There come times when I have*
> *nothing more to tell God.*
>
> *If I were to continue to pray in words,*
> *I would have to repeat*
> *what I have already said.*

> *At such times it is wonderful to say to God,*
> *'May I be in Thy presence, Lord?*
>
> *I have nothing more to say to Thee,*
> *but I do love to be in Thy presence.'"*

———

> *"As white snowflakes fall quietly*
> *and thickly on a winter day,*
> *answers to prayer*
> *will settle down upon you*
> *at every step you take,*
> *even to your dying day.*
>
> *The story of your life*
> *will be the story of prayer*
> *and answers to prayer."*

William Temple (& Edith Schaeffer's) Prayer Truth:

God Makes *"Coincidences"* Happen When We Pray

One of the most accurate observances ever made, was penned by Anglican Archbishop of Canterbury William Temple (1881-1944):

> *"When I pray coincidences happen,*
> *and when I don't, they don't."*

This is also the message, with example after example, of another of my all-time favorite books:

L'Abri
by Edith Schaeffer.

She was married to Francis Schaeffer. Together they founded an amazing "living on faith" Christian ministry in French Switzerland called *L'Abri* (French, meaning: *The Shelter*).

Edith Schaeffer was born in China to parents who were missionaries with Hudson Taylor's *China Inland Mission* (Ruth Graham, wife of World Evangelist Billy Graham, was also born in China, the daughter of Presbyterian Medical Missionary, L. Nelson Bell).

L'Abri

In 1955, Francis and Edith Schaeffer left a Presbyterian Pastorate in St. Louis, Missouri, and founded the *L'Abri Fellowship* in French Switzerland as a Christian teaching and witnessing Community, supported through "living by prayer."

They did not ask anyone for funding, but only prayed to God for it.

Francis Schaeffer wrote twenty books. Edith Schaeffer wrote more than two dozen.

The God Who is There is one of the books in Francis Shaeffer's popular Trilogy, portraying the history of European culture in religion, art, music, philosophy and science.

Schaeffer explains how historic Western culture gradually changed from a Christian worldview to its current non-Christian perspective.

Consistently Answered Prayer

L'Abri Fellowship was created as a ministry to present the Gospel through a comparative discussion of philosophy and religion.

The book illustrates "living on faith" by showing how God consistently answered their prayers in their day to day lives.

The stated purpose of the *L'Abri* ministry:

"To show forth by demonstration,
in our life and work,
the existence of God."

Reading the book *L'Abri* is a great blessing. We recommend it as a perfect companion to E.M. Bounds' *Power Through Prayer*.

It is the practical outworking of what is found in Bounds' teaching, as seen in the Schaeffers' almost daily receiving of answers to their prayers.

The book *L'Abri* is so wonderful, because it shows the warmth and joy of actually *living* the Christian life, not just *talking* about it. The Schaeffer's amazing early ministry at *L'Abri* was, and still is, a great inspiration to our own ministry.

S.G. Preston

A Personal Prayer Tip:

Praying a Psalm You Are Memorizing Is Pure Joy

As Lay Monks, many of us spend an hour a day; some, three or more hours a day in prayer; often either praying psalms that we have previously memorized, or memorizing new ones.

In the latter case, we are praying them in an attitude of prayer, even as we are memorizing them. This can be done for any length of time.

To many, an entire hour each day may seem like too long a time to spend in prayer.

For those who have prayed a dedicated hour a day for several decades, it is more likely to seem too short, and over much too quickly.

See What Works Best for You

Of course, the hour can be divided into two separate half hours of prayer, three twenty minute time periods of prayer, or in other ways.

For some, it may be much more difficult to try to continue your daily hour of prayer later in the day, because there are so many distractions and interruptions.

But if this works for you, well and good.

Praying at St. Paul's Cathedral

We have already seen that many men and women of God in the past have dedicated a daily hour, or even more, each day to prayer.

Canon H.P. Liddon (1829-1890) cites the example of Anglican Bishop Andrewes (1555-1626), one of the early Protestant Reformers in England.

Liddon served as the Canon, or Priest, of St. Paul's Cathedral in London. We were blessed to be able to pray in the Prayer Chapel there.

While at St. Paul's, Fr. Liddon drew 3-4,000 people regularly into the Cathedral, to hear his preaching.

Later, as a conservative Theologian, he became Professor of Holy Scripture Exegesis at Oxford University.

Canon Liddon's Prayer Truth:

Prayer Helps Us Understand God's Word

Canon Liddon is in agreement with Evagrius of Pontus' often repeated statement, which we have already looked at, but which is worth looking at again here:

> *"A theologian is one who prays;*
> *and one who prays is a theologian."*

Canon Liddon tells us:

> *"The great masters and teachers*
> *in Christian doctrine*
> *have always found in prayer,*
> *their highest source*
> *of illumination.*
>
> *Not to go beyond the limits of the English Church,*
> *it is recorded of Bishop Andrewes that*
> *he spent five hours daily on his knees.*
>
> *The greatest practical resolves*
> *that enriched and beautified*
> *human life in Christian times*
> *have been arrived at*
> *in prayer."*

Richard Newton

Why have these men and women of God spent so much time in prayer? Why may we need to spend more time in prayer than we do now?

Richard Newton (1813-1887) has given us one answer. He was called *"The Prince of Preachers to the Young"* by Charles Spurgeon, *"The Prince of Preachers."*

Newton was famous in his lifetime for his highly effective sermons to children. Christian children's books that he wrote in the 1800's are still in print today.

146

S.G. Preston

Richard Newton's Prayer Tip:

Prayer Makes Life Easier

Richard Newton confessed that, as hard as it sometimes was for him to pray, he found that it made the rest of his life easier:

"The principal cause
of my leanness
and unfruitfulness
is owing to an unaccountable
backwardness to pray.

I can write, or read, or converse,
or hear with a ready heart;
but prayer is more spiritual
and inward than any of these,
and the more spiritual
any duty is,
the more my carnal heart
is apt to start from it.

Prayer and patience and faith
are never disappointed.

I have long since learned
that if ever
I was to be a minister,
faith and prayer
must make me one.

When I can find my heart
in frame and liberty for prayer,
everything else
is comparatively easy."

6.4 Memorize Scripture to Worship God

"But without faith it is impossible
to please Him.

For those who come to God
must believe that He is,
and that He is a rewarder
of those who diligently
seek Him."

-Hebrews 11:6

———

"Cleachtadh a dheanann maistreacht."

"Practice makes mastery."

-Old Gaelic Saying

Reasons To Memorize Scripture

We read the Bible to learn about God. God reveals Himself to us through His Word. He also reveals His will for our lives: how we should live, and what He wants us to do.

"For I know the plans I have for you,
declares the Lord,
plans to prosper you
and not to harm you,
plans to give you
hope and a future."

-Jeremiah 29:11 (NIV)

We memorize Scripture to internalize the truth of God's Word into our minds and hearts, and to grow in the knowledge of God.

We memorize Scripture to better share the Good News of Christ's Salvation to a lost world; obeying our Lord's command to fulfill Christ's Great Commission.

S.G. Preston

To know God's Will and Live God's Way

*"The entrance of Your word
gives light.*

*It gives understanding
to the naive."*

-Psalm 119:130

To Be Declared Holy Through God's Grace

*"Sanctify them
through Your truth."*

-John 17:17

Definition of *sanctify*:

*"Set apart as, or declare holy;
consecrate; free from sin,
purify."*

To Be Better Able to Share God's Truth

*"Study to show yourself
approved by God,
a workman
that needs not
to be ashamed,
correctly teaching
the word
of truth."*

-2 Timothy 2:15

We Memorize Psalms for Use In Prayer

The Psalms cover every need in prayer of the human condition, and contain the solutions to the very problems that we are praying about.

Along with *The Lord's Prayer,* they are God's own instructions of how and what to pray:

*"Speaking to yourselves in psalms
and hymns and spiritual songs;
singing and making melody in
your heart to the Lord."*

-Ephesians 5:19

——

*"Let everything that has breath praise the LORD.
Praise the LORD."*

-Psalm 150:6

A Personal Prayer Tip:

Prayer is Much More than Just Asking For Things

The greatest blessing that God can give us is Himself; a closer relationship with Him, and the revelation of the knowledge of Himself.

All three Persons of the Trinity are always involved in our prayer life. We receive everything from the Father, in the Name of and through the intercession of Jesus Christ, by the Holy Spirit.

*"The Lord is near to all that call upon Him;
to all that call upon Him in truth."*

-Psalm 145:18

Prayer is not primarily about asking for things, but about developing and growing in a relationship of communion with God through Christ.

There is a Scripture that conveys this so well, that I chose it as one of the first three verses comprising the Rule of our Lay Monastic Order, *The Celtic Cross Rule*:

*"Draw near to God,
and He will draw near to you."*

-James 4:8

150

6.5 Memorize Scripture: Share Christ, Resist Temptation

*"Is trom an t-ualach
an t-aineaolas."*

*"Ignorance is a
heavy burden."*

-Old Gaelic Saying

———

*"An te nach gcuireann san earrach
ni bhaineann se san fhomhar."*

*"Whoever does not plant in the spring,
will not reap in the fall."*

-Old Gaelic Saying

Your Word Have I Hidden in My Heart

It may not have occurred to us to think of memorizing Scripture as a way of improving our prayer life.

Yet this was the practice of the leaders of the Early Church. It was the practice of the leaders of the Protestant Reformation.

During the many centuries in between, it was also the practice of the humble Celtic Christian monks in Ireland, throughout the British Isles, and on continental Europe.

Be Ready Always

When we think about memorizing Scripture, we often think of it in relation to sharing the Gospel with others.

We are talking to a friend or acquaintance about Christ, and a question arises. We want to share a particular verse, but can't remember the exact wording.

We try to look it up in the Bible, but we can't find it. Later, we search a Concordance and memorize it, so we will be ready next time.

We are Applying 1 Peter 3:15

*"But sanctify the Lord God
in your hearts.*

*Be ready always to give an answer
to everyone who asks you,*

*a reason for the hope
that is in you,
with humility
and reverence."*

That I Might Not Sin Against You

Another reason we will memorize a verse, is for use against a particular temptation. Our Lord, resisting with Scripture the temptations of the Devil in the desert wilderness, is our example.

This is an excellent reason to commit God's Word to memory. The operative verse here is:

*"Your word have I
hidden in my heart;
that I might not sin
against You."*

-Psalm 119:11

John 3:16

Most of us, when we begin memorizing scripture for the benefit of our prayer life, will start off with the teaching of Christ and learn by heart *The Lord's Prayer.*

I memorized it as a child without ever trying, just by hearing it in Church during every service.

We may also memorize John 3:16. Many raised in Evangelical homes memorize this verse as the very first one that they learn, often between the ages of three and six.

Unfortunately, this is where many of us stop, but we shouldn't.

Prayers in the New Testament

There are several excellent prayers of the Apostle Paul found in his Letters. Three of them are found, respectively, in his Letters to the Ephesians, Philippians, and Colossians.

When I pray these New Testament prayers, I simply change the tenses (*your* to *our*; *you* to *we*; *His* to *You, Your*) to make them my own personal prayers to God.

I began memorizing and praying these Bible prayers in my early twenties, but you could just write them out, to pray them without memorizing them first.

Paul's Prayer from Ephesians 3:14-21

"For this reason, I bow my knees to You,
the Father of our Lord Jesus Christ:

from You the whole family
in heaven and earth is named;

that You would grant us,
according to the riches of Your glory,

to be strengthened with might through Your Spirit
in our innermost self.

That Christ may dwell in our hearts through faith.

That we, being rooted and grounded in love,
may be able to comprehend with all the saints,
what is the width and length and depth and height,
and to know the love of Christ,
which surpasses all knowledge.

That we may be filled with all the fullness of God.

Now to You who are able to do exceedingly abundantly
above all that we ask or think,
according to the Power that works in us;

to You be glory in the Church by Christ Jesus
to all generations,
forever and ever.
Amen."

Prayer for Love, Knowledge, Judgment, Deliverance from Sin, & Manifesting the Fruit of the Spirit: Found in Philippians 1:9-11

"And this I pray,
that our love may abound yet more and more,
in knowledge and in all judgment.

That we may discern which things are the best,
from among those that differ.

That we may be sincere and without offence
until the day of Christ;

being filled with the fruits of righteousness,
which are by Jesus Christ,
to the glory and praise of God."

Prayer to Know God's Will, Aid Our Christian Walk, Experience Joy in Our Christian Life: Recorded In Colossians 1:9-11

"For this cause we also, since the day we heard it,
do not cease to pray,

and to desire that we might be filled
with the knowledge of Your will,
in all wisdom and spiritual understanding.

That we might walk worthy of You, Lord,
in all ways pleasing to You,
being fruitful in every good work,
and increasing in the knowledge of You;

strengthened with all might,
according to Your glorious power,
in all patience and endurance
with joyfulness..."

6.6 Memorize Scripture for a Deeper Prayer Life

"Tada gan iarracht."

"Nothing without effort."

-Old Gaelic Saying

――

"Chan ann leis a'chiad bhuille thuiteas a'chraobh."

"It is not with the first stroke that the tree falls."

-Old Gaelic Saying

Memorizing Psalms

We are told in the book of Acts that the calling of the leaders of the early Church was to prayer, and to the ministry of the Word (Acts 6:4).

We believe that this is the calling of *all* Christians. That the Apostles are our example in this.

Bishops in the first centuries after Christ were required to memorize all 150 Psalms.

In Ireland 1,400 years ago, in small stone Oratories, communities of twelve dedicated monks gathered daily for the reading of the Gospel.

They did not gather for the reading of the Psalms, for like the Bishops of the Early Church, each monk had the entire Book of Psalms committed to memory.

Some of the early Irish Celtic monks in Ireland prayed all 150 Psalms once through every day! Most Christian monks throughout history have prayed them through once a week.

Today, many Christians throughout the world have decided to pray through five Psalms every day; praying through all 150 of them each month.

We have seen how William Wilberforce (1759-1833), a godly Christian; and aided by *Amazing Grace* composer John Newton; was the man most responsible for getting the British Parliament to abolish the slave trade throughout the British Empire.

Visiting London's Regency Park Zoo

Wilberforce once spoke about a time when he was walking along Baker Street toward London's Regency Park.

This sticks in my mind, because Linda and I have walked along this same street to Regency Park (it is also where the fictional Sherlock Holmes' address of 221B Baker Street is located).

We were going to the Regency Park Zoo, because it had always been a dream of Lay Monk Bob's to go there, but he had never had the opportunity to actually do so.

We went in his place, videotaping our visit, and he was very happy to watch it when we returned.

Memorizing Psalm 119

Wilberforce said that while he walked down Baker Street, he prayed through the entire Psalm 119. Praying a psalm or psalms, is a wonderful way to pray and redeem our time.

Psalm 119 is the longest psalm in the Bible; fourteen pages long in most Bible versions.

This makes me wonder just how much of the Bible William Wilberforce must have had memorized!

David Livingstone (1813-1872), an early missionary and one of the first explorers in Africa, was another who had learned Psalm 119 by heart.

Memorizing Psalm 23

I myself often pray psalms that I have memorized; while driving around doing errands, and especially when waiting in lines; such as at the bank or supermarket, or at a Doctor's or Dentist's office.

I will always remember how happy a young woman named Linda was, after I had encouraged her to memorize Psalm 23. I would later marry her.

She told me that it was so wonderful how the Lord kept bringing this Psalm to her mind, many times throughout the day.

6.7 Praying for an Hour, Drawing Near to Christ

*"It takes us long
to learn that prayer is
more important than organization,
more powerful than armies,
more influential than wealth,
and mightier than
all learning."*

-Samuel Chadwick (1860-1932)
English Methodist Pastor
Author: *The Path of Prayer*

The Bible Teaches Many Types of Prayer

*Petition, Praise,
Intercession, Adoration,
Silent Stillness, Thanksgiving,
Deep Meditation On His Word.*

There can be bliss in prayer. There can be agony in prayer. Sometimes it is simply the hardest work that you have ever done.

I have written that when I first became a Christian and prayed for an hour, more often than not it was intense travail and tedium, as if each hour of prayer lasted for several days.

The Joy of the Lord

I can still recall times when the entire first hour might pass before the Spirit of God broke through, and the presence of God was felt.

Today, the opposite happens, and an hour passes, sometime three hours or more; seeming like only five or ten minutes.

I am torn, almost physically inside, as I realize I have to *stop praying* and start my work on the other requirements of the day.

Our wonderful, glorious God, grants the gift of joy to His children. It is the awareness of His presence, and of His great love for us, that brings us this joy.

William Wilberforce Wrote:

*"This perpetual hurry
of business and company
ruins me in soul, if not in body.*

More solitude and earlier hours!

*I suspect I have been allotting habitually
too little time to religious exercises,
such as private devotion
and religious meditation,
Scripture-reading, etc.*

Hence, I am lean and cold and hard.

*I had better allot two hours
or an hour and a half daily.*

*I have been keeping
too late hours,
and hence have had
but a hurried half hour
in a morning to myself.*

*Surely the experience
of all good men
confirms the proposition
that without a due measure
of private devotions,
the soul will grow lean.*

*But all may be done
through prayer --
almighty prayer,
I am ready to say --
and why not?*

*For that it is almighty
is only through
the gracious ordination
of the God of love and truth.*

O then; pray, pray, pray!"

S.G. Preston

An Hour of Prayer With Fasting

In New Testament times, the Jewish people fasted on Tuesdays and Thursdays. The Early Church, to differentiate, fasted on Wednesdays and Fridays.

Christ instructed us (Boldface mine):

*"Moreover, **when** you fast…"*

Fasting seems to *intensify* prayer, because it removes some of the distractions that we are prone to. What C.S. Lewis once said about prayer, is also true about fasting. Fasting does not change God; it changes *us*.

1931 - O. Hallesby Writes His Book On Prayer

In his inspiring book, *Prayer*, O. Hallesby teaches:

"The purpose of fasting
is to loosen
to some degree
the ties which bind us to
the world of material things
and our surroundings
as a whole,

in order that we may
concentrate all our
spiritual powers
upon the unseen
and eternal
things."

Acts 3:12 informs us:

"As they ministered
to the Lord,
and fasted,
the Holy Spirit said…"

159

An Hour of Prayer With the Word of God

The joy of praying psalms. The Book of Psalms is quoted in the New Testament more than any other Old Testament book. It is quoted by Christ more than any other Old Testament book.

The Psalms have such a great appeal to us because they speak of Christ, reveal the Father, and are used by the Holy Spirit to teach us how to pray: to enter into the very presence of God.

This message, found in the Psalms and throughout the New Testament, can be seen in some of the Responses below:

Officiant: *"God is our refuge and strength, a very present help in trouble. Therefore we shall not fear."* (Psalms 46:1-10)

All: *"There is no fear in love, for perfect love casts out fear."* (1 John 4:18)

Officiant: *"Having therefore boldness to enter into the Holy of Holies, by the blood of Jesus:"* (Hebrews 10:19)

All: *"Let us then go boldly to the throne of grace, so that we can receive mercy, and find grace to help in time of need."* (Hebrews 4:16)

All Scripture Is Truth, Inspired by God

Through His Word, God reveals Himself to us. We should be open to the guidance of the Holy Spirit, judged always by God's written Word, because all Scripture is inspired by God:

"All Scripture is given
by inspiration of God,
and is profitable
for doctrine, for reproof,
for correction,
for instruction
in righteousness:"

2 Timothy 3:16

———

*"In hope of
eternal life,
which God,
who cannot lie,
promised before
the world began;"*

-Titus 1:2

——

"Your word is truth."

John 17:17

The Authority of the Holy Scriptures

If we are comparing and contrasting two different sources of information, and one of the sources is God's *Holy Scriptures*, which we know to be *absolute truth*; then it logically and of necessity becomes our *ultimate and final authority*.

Between 175 and 185 A.D., St. Irenaeus, the Greek Bishop of Lyon, France wrote in his book, *Against Heresies*:

*"We have learned
the plan of our salvation
from no one else
other than from
those through whom
the Gospel
has come down to us.*

*For they did at one time
proclaim the Gospel in public.*

*And at a later period, by the
will of God,
they handed the Gospel
down to us in the Scriptures --
to be... 'the ground and pillar
of our faith.'"*

161

All These Things Happened for Our Example, and Were Written for Our Instruction (1 Corinthians 10:11)

"But the days will come,
when the Bridegroom
shall be taken away from them,
and then shall they fast
in those days."

-Luke 5:35

———

"And she was a widow,
about eighty-four years old,
who departed not from the Temple
but served God with fastings and prayers
night and day."

-Luke 2:37

*   *   *

S.G. Preston

Ephesians for Today's Prayer Warriors

"You therefore endure hardness, as a good soldier of Jesus Christ.

No one that wars entangles themselves with the affairs of this life,
that they may please Him who has chosen them to be a soldier."

-2 Timothy 2:3-4

The Full Armor of God

It is believed by many that when Paul wrote about *the full armor of God*, he was making his spiritual point while describing the armor and weaponry of a Roman soldier of his era; *perhaps the one who was standing guard over Paul at the time!*

To we who live in modern times, swords and shields have a romantic quality (think of King Arthur and Robin Hood) that would never have occurred to Christians living in Paul's own time.

I composed the following *"today's rendition"* of Ephesians 6:14-18 in 2006, to help put Paul's words more into the historical context in which they were written. We should never forget that we are in a *spiritual war*.

A Version of Ephesians 6:14-18 for Today's Soldiers

"Stand therefore, having your waist girded about
with the cartridge belt of truth;
having on the flak-jacket of righteousness,
and your feet shod with the combat boots
of the preparation of the gospel of peace.

Above all, taking the air-cover of faith,
wherewith you shall be able to quench all the
fiery incoming missiles of the wicked.

And take the helmet of salvation,
and the automatic rifle of the Spirit, which is the Word of God:
maintaining constant contact with Command Central

by praying always with all prayer and supplication in the Spirit,
and watching with all perseverance and supplication
for all your fellow soldiers..."

163

Answers to Prayer
PrayerFoundation ™ 24-Hr. Prayerchain

July 7, 2006 - Answer to Prayer

Dear *Prayer Warriors*,
Praise our wonderful, wonderful, Lord Jesus Christ!

I requested prayers for my husband, who is Chieftain of his Clan. He was banned from village, because he stood up for one of village youths involved in brawl.

The youth was fined a very ridiculous amount. There was no way he could possibly pay fine. Much of village laws still practiced, belongs to dark ages. My husband preached Jesus into the Council Meeting in way of reforming some of these laws. Has made many enemies since involved in village affairs.

However, your prayers were answered, and even though he did not agree to the penalty, and ban, but he obeyed the law. He rounded up his family, and raised the amount for the fine.

On delivering it, the council were emotional, and thanked him for his godly wisdom, and pardoned all the Chiefs, totaling six, who had also been banned from village. Some had been out for several years, but because of my husband, they received pardon. It was truly an emotional time.

Praise, glory, and honour, be returned to our heavenly Father!

Thank you for your faithful service for our Lord Jesus Christ!

-Tifi (Samoa)

(From the book: *Answers to Prayer* by S.G. Preston)

7. *The Threefold Daily Prayers*

7.1 3 p.m.: Psalm 117

"Bishop Epiphanius of Cyprus was told by the Abbot
of a monastery that the Bishop
supported in Palestine:

'Because of your prayers for us, we do not neglect
our appointed round of psalms.

We are always careful to recite Terce,
(the Third Hour; 9 a.m.)
Sext (the Sixth Hour; Noon),
and None (the Ninth Hour, 3 p.m.).

Epiphanius answered the Abbot by saying:

'It is obvious that you do not bother
about the other hours of the day,
if you cease from prayer.

True monks have prayer and the Psalms
continually in their heart.'"

-Sayings of the Desert Fathers

3 p.m.

Entering our Chapel, I light a candle. It is now 3 p.m. I drop down on my knees and make the Sign of the Cross simultaneously as I pray:

"In the Name of the Father, and of the Son,
and of the Holy Spirit."

Continuing, I pray the entire Psalm 117:

"O praise the LORD, all ye nations: praise Him, all ye people.
For His merciful kindness is great toward us,
and the truth of the LORD endureth forever.
Praise ye the LORD."

Why Pray The Threefold Daily Prayers?

As Christians, we are exhorted by our Lord to: *"...pray always..."*

Why then would I pray specifically at 3 p.m.? Why would I also pray at 9 a.m. and at Noon?

> *"Therefore, it is well to let prayer*
> *be the first employment in the early morning,*
> *and the last in the evening.*
>
> *Avoid diligently those false*
> *and deceptive thoughts which say,*
>
> *'Wait a little, I will pray an hour hence;*
> *I must perform this or that.'*
>
> *For with such thoughts*
> *a man quits prayer for business,*
> *which lays hold of and entangles him*
> *so that he comes not to pray*
> *the whole day long..."*

-Martin Luther (1483-15460

Why Did the Apostles Pray at: 9 a.m., Noon, & 3 p.m?

I began the practice of praying what I call *The Threefold Daily Prayers*, because one day while reading the Bible, a question suddenly occurred to me:

> *In the New Testament, why did the Apostles pray at*
> *the specific times of 9 a.m., Noon, and 3 p.m.?*

Even at the time, I realized that this would seem like a very strange question to most Protestants. Strange that it was even being asked!

I no longer remember what year this happened, when I started observing them daily; but I began posting articles on *The Threefold Daily Prayers*, the Scriptures where they are found, and the testimonies of ancient Christian writers concerning them; on the website of the *PrayerFoundation,*™ when we began it in 1999.

S.G. Preston

Unknown to Protestants

Protestantism has been in existence for 500 years. Hundreds of Denominations and tens of thousands of independent Protestant Churches have been founded during this time.

Yet had *even one* of these Churches, in all of the entire 500 years, ever observed these three daily times of prayer that are recorded as being observed by the Apostles in the New Testament?

I admit I may have missed it somehow, but when we began our ministry in 1999, I had never heard of even *one* such Protestant church, and I had been a student of Religious History and Church History for all of my adult life! In fact, Religious History was my area of study at both a secular University and a Christian Bible College.

The closest and only example I could even think of, was that Anglican Churches observe Morning and Evening Prayer Services, and Lutheran Churches recommend Morning and Evening individual and family prayer.

Three Specific Times for Prayer

As a Lay monastic Order, we have chosen to pray certain Scriptures as prayers at these special times, but this is just the particular practice of our Order.

When we are able to, we pray The Lord's Prayer at 9 a.m., The 23rd Psalm at Noon, and Psalm 117 at 3 p.m. Then we pray whatever else we may be led to pray.

The Early Church seems to have begun each of the three prayer times with The Lord's Prayer. They could then, as they were led and as time allowed, add spontaneous prayer, as the Scripture says:

> *"Speaking to yourselves in psalms and hymns*
> *and spiritual songs, singing and making melody*
> *in your heart to the Lord;*
>
> *Giving thanks always for all things to God the Father*
> *in the Name of our Lord Jesus Christ..."*

-Ephesians 5:19-20

Observed in the Old & New Testaments, & by the Early Church

Yes, these three daily times of prayer were observed by David and Daniel in the Old Testament, by the Jewish people, by the Apostles in the New Testament, and by the early Christians. Their practice was continued by all Christians for the first several centuries of the Early Church.

At that time, their continued observance was relegated to the practice of the monastics, who have never ceased observing them up to this very day, in both the Eastern Orthodox and Roman Catholic Churches.

Yet most Protestants seem never to have even heard of them.

Referred to in the New Testament

When I mentioned these three Biblical times of prayer to Christian friends, they actually seemed to get mad, and said that they didn't believe me!

They said they knew that there was *no such thing* in the New Testament, because they had been Christians for forty years, had read the Bible and attended Church all of that time, and *had never heard even once* of any such thing as three specific times of prayer in the New Testament!

When I showed them the specific Scripture verses that refer to these three prayer times in the New Testament, they acted like they didn't know what to think.

As though I was pulling some kind of trick on them, and they just needed to know from a Christian Teacher or Pastor how to explain it all away.

Evening, and Morning, and at Noon

There are also two mentions in the Old Testament of these three prayer times, though only Noon is given as a *specific* time, the other two times of prayer are referred to simply as *Evening* and *Morning* in Psalm 55:17.

Daniel 6:10 is the other Old Testament Scripture where they are referred to.

Why Don't Protestants Observe Them?

The mentions in the New Testament of these special times of prayer will be discussed, one by one, at some length later in this book. My first question was followed almost immediately in my mind by a second question.

Why don't Protestants observe them?

Well, of course, I considered, the Apostles were all *Jewish*. They observed many things found in the Law of Moses that Gentile Christians do not.

We do not follow the Jewish dietary rules regarding what and what not to eat. Neither do we celebrate the holidays in the Old Testament.

We do not keep the Law, for Christ's death on the cross has ended its required observance for those who are Christians, whether Jewish or Gentiles.

Colossians 2:14 explains:

> *"Blotting out*
> *the handwriting*
> *of ordinances*
> *that was against us,*
> *which was contrary to us,*
> *and took it out of the way,*
> *nailing it to His cross..."*

Why Did the Old Testament Saints Observe These Three Times of Prayer?

Where are they to be found in the Law of Moses?

I could not remember ever reading any mention of them there, and for good reason: these three special times of prayer are not a part of the Mosaic Law.

Were they then some of the extra-biblical observances that the Pharisees had devised, and which Christ had condemned?

Of course, they are not extra-biblical. As we have seen, they are mentioned twice in the Old Testament.

169

1,000 Years Before the Pharisees

Another problem with the Pharisee theory, is that they had been practiced by Old Testament believers for at least a thousand years before the Pharisees even existed.

There is yet a third problem with this view: these three times of prayer at 9 a.m., Noon, and 3 p.m. are observed by the Apostles *after* Christ's Resurrection.

The Apostles had followed Christ's teaching in rejecting Pharisaic extra-Biblical regulations, even when Christ was still with them, *before* His Crucifixion.

Why Did the Reformers Reject These Three Prayer Times?

Knowing what the Protestant Reformers had taught in this area, would no doubt clear up the mystery of 500 years of neglect by Protestants, of an Apostolic practice recorded in the New Testament and observed by the Early Church *for hundreds of years*.

This subject must already have been dealt with during the Protestant Reformation. I only needed to research what the response of the Reformers had been.

As they say, why try to *re-invent the wheel?*

7.2 Rejected by the Protestant Reformers

"We may be sure that...
the blindness about which posterity will ask,

"But how could they have thought that?"

-- lies where we never suspected it...

None of us can fully escape this blindness,
but we shall certainly increase it...
if we read only modern books.

Where they are true they will give us truths
which we half knew already.

Where they are false they will aggravate
the error with which we are already
dangerously ill.

The only palliative is to keep
the clean sea breeze of the centuries
blowing through our minds,

and this can be done only
by reading old books."

-C.S. Lewis (1898-1963)
From his Introduction to:
On the Incarnation by St. Athanasius

The Reformers Reject Praying at 9 a.m., Noon, and 3 p.m.

In fact, the Protestant Reformers seem to have considered the practice of praying at certain times of the day, to have been a creation of the Church hierarchy in the Middle Ages.

They seem to have rejected it on that basis.

As previously mentioned, the Church of England (Anglican Church) and the Lutheran Churches did retain Morning and Evening times of prayer.

But even they also rejected *The Threefold Daily Prayer* times of 9 a.m., Noon, and 3 p.m.

1566 - Heinrich Bullinger Writes The Second Helvetic Confession

Fairly representative of the view of all of the Reformers, is that put forth in *The Second Helvetic Confession*. It is used in Reformed Churches.

This Confession was composed by Heinrich Bullinger, the successor to Swiss Reformer Ulrich Zwingli. Bullinger states in Chapter XXIII:

"Canonical hours
are not prescribed in the Scriptures,
and are unknown to antiquity."

Canons are the ecclesiastical rules that were established by Church Councils. The Canonical Hours are certain times of prayer specified in Canon Law. The number of such officially Church sanctioned times of prayer has varied throughout history.

Bullinger was likely referring to the seven times of prayer generally observed in the monasteries of his time.

Reformers Unaware of 2nd Century Church Manuals

We now know from second century Church manuals: the *Didache* and the *Canons of Hippolytus,* that even the four *additional* times of canonical prayer (making seven total) can be traced back to the early Christians of the second century, and their meetings in the Catacombs of Rome.

The Reformers were unfortunately unaware of the existence of these manuals, because they were not re-discovered or available in translation until the 1800's.

The Canonical times of prayer were not the creation, hundreds years after the time of the early Christians, of the Church Councils of the fourth and fifth centuries.

Neither were they created by the medieval Church hierarchy, an additional seven hundred years beyond that (1,000 years and more after the time of the New Testament and the Early Church).

These historic seven times of prayer, observed by the Early Church in the Catacombs of Rome, *include* the three Apostolic prayer times.

S.G. Preston

King James Version

The *King James Version* of the New Testament refers to these three times of prayer as *the third hour, the sixth hour,* and *the ninth hour* of the day, in the *Gospels of Matthew, Mark,* and *Luke.*

They were part of the *Jewish* numbering of the hours of the day, counting from sunrise, roughly 6 a.m.

The *Gospel of John* instead uses the *Roman* numbering of the hours of the day.

In Latin, the words for third, sixth, and ninth; are *Terce, Sext,* and *None.*

These Latin terms are how you will often find these three times of prayer mentioned in historical works, as well as in popular books, movies, and on television.

Bullinger: Canonical Hours Not Prescribed In Scripture

The word "prescribed" has several different meanings.

We are all familiar with: *"A Doctor writing a prescription."*

Another meaning implies a *command*:

> *"To state
> authoritatively
> or as a rule
> that an action
> or procedure
> should be
> carried out."*

And a third meaning implies *a recommendation*:

> *"To recommend
> a substance
> or action
> as something
> beneficial."*

Bullinger: Canonical Hours Unknown to Antiquity

Leaving aside the additional four times of prayer mentioned in the Church Canons (which are not found in the New Testament, and therefore we are not concerned with here), Bullinger was correct in saying that these three prayer times of Nine a.m., Noon, and Three p.m., are not *"prescribed"* in the Scriptures.

If he meant that their observance is nowhere *"commanded, enjoined, or otherwise required"* by any believers, either in the Old Testament or in the New Testament.

However, I do believe that he was mistaken when he said that they were *"unknown to antiquity."*

7.3 Unknown to Antiquity?

*"Not, of course, that there is
any magic about the past.*

*People were no cleverer then
than they are now.*

*They made
as many mistakes as we.*

But not the same mistakes.

*They will not flatter us
in the errors
we're already committing,
and their own errors,
being now open
and palpable,
will not endanger us."*

-C.S. Lewis (1898-1963)

Tertullian, Origen, and Clement of Alexandria

The Protestant Reformer Heinrich Bullinger can hardly be faulted for being unaware of the existence of the late first, or early second century Church manuals: the *Didache* and the *Canons of Hippolytus.*

As I have said earlier, *The Didache* was not even discovered, and *The Canons of Hippolytus* not readily available in vernacular translation, until the 1800's.

By that time, the Lutheran, Calvinist, Anabaptist, and Anglican Churches had already been in existence for over 300 years, and had rejected observance of the three special Early Church prayer times for that entire period.

It does seem that Bullinger was mistaken in his contention that these three times of prayer observed by the Early Church were *"unknown to antiquity,"* since they are mentioned in both the Old and New Testaments. They are also mentioned in the third century Christian writings of Tertullian, Origen, and Clement of Alexandria.

175

The Practice of the Apostles

It is possible, however, that even if the Early Church manuals had been discovered and made available three centuries earlier, they would have had little influence on the Reformers.

I say this because the Reformers, several of which had formerly been Catholic priests, should have been familiar with the writings of Tertullian, Origen, and Clement of Alexandria.

And I also say this, because even the practice of the Apostles in the New Testament failed to persuade them to retain these three times of prayer: the heritage and practice of the first several centuries of the entire Christian Church.

International Standard Bible Encyclopedia

What then is the history of, and is there any Scriptural warrant for the observance of these three times of prayer?

The International Standard Bible Encyclopedia (1915); Orr, James, M.A., D.D., General Editor; "Entry for: '*Hours of Prayer*'" (by Henry E. Dosker); informs us of these three prayer times that:

> *"The first coincided*
> *with the morning sacrifice,*
> *at the 3rd hour of the morning,*
> *at 9 a.m. therefore.*
> (Acts 2:15)

> *The second was at the 6th hour,*
> *or at noon,*
> *and may have coincided with the*
> *thanksgiving for the chief meal of the day,*
> *a religious custom*
> *apparently universally observed.*
> (Matthew 15:36; Acts 27:35)

> *The 3rd hour of prayer coincided*
> *with the evening sacrifice,*
> *at the 9th Hour.*
> (3:00 p.m.)"

176

David

Exactly when these three times of prayer first began to be observed by the Jewish people is not known, but we have already learned that their earliest mention in the Bible was made by David.

> *"Evening, and morning, and at noon: I will pray,*
> *and call out loud, and He shall hear my voice."*

-Psalm 55:17

King David's reign was c. 1000 B.C. Four hundred years later, we again find three times of prayer mentioned, in the Book of Daniel (Daniel 6:10), where we learn that the Prophet Daniel was thrown into a den of lions because of his faithfulness in their observance:

> *"Now when Daniel knew that the writing was signed,*
> *he went into his house, and his windows*
> *being open in his chamber toward Jerusalem,*
> *he kneeled upon his knees three times a day,*
> *and prayed, and gave thanks before his God,*
> *as he had done before."*

-Daniel 6:10

Daniel and David

We do not know Daniel's exact birth and death dates.

We do know that he was a young man when Nebuchadnezzar conquered Jerusalem in 607 B.C., and carried him off in captivity to Babylon. We also know that Daniel was still living 70 years later when the Persian Emperor Cyrus conquered Babylon in 537 B.C.

In the books of Holy Scripture that Daniel had available to him around 607 B.C., there is only *one* mention of *praying three times a day*; by Psalmist and prophet King David; but observing this practice was so important to Daniel, that he was willing to die rather than give it up.

It is only reasonable to think that Daniel, praying three times a day in his own prayer life, was following David's Biblical example.

The Apostles and the Early Church

Christians are encouraged to pray not only at certain times of day, but at *all times*. Romans 12:12 exhorts us to *"be instant in prayer."* In the King James Version's older English, *"instant"* means: *"constant, consistent, persistent."*

Yet we learn from history and from the New Testament that, like David and Daniel, the Early Church also prayed at these same three times of day; and that the Early Church was following the example of the Apostles.

7.4 The Testimony of Antiquity: Early Christian Writings

"Prayer should not be regarded as a duty
which must be performed, but rather as a privilege to be enjoyed,
a rare delight that is always revealing some new beauty."

-E.M. Bounds (1835-1913)

Late 100's A.D. - The Didache

The observance of The Threefold Daily Prayers by the Early Church is taught in *The Didache*: or, *The Teaching of the Twelve Apostles*. It was not written by the Apostles themselves, but is said to present their teachings.

The *Didache,* a Church manual from the late first, or early second century, is mentioned in Eusebius' *History of the Church: From Christ to Constantine* (written c. 240-c. 260 A.D.).

Eusebius was the first Christian Historian; his book is the earliest historical work recording the history of Christianity *after* the New Testament.

c. 200 A.D. - Tertullian

The observance of the three special times of prayer is also mentioned by Tertullian, writing around 200 A.D., in Chapter 25 of: *On Prayer*.

Tertullian speaks of the Christians of his time praying before meals, before going to the public baths, and at sunrise and sunset; but he finds a special solemnity in the Scriptures for these three particular times of prayer:

"Touching the time, however,
the extrinsic observance of certain hours
will not be unprofitable.
Those common hours, I mean,
which mark the intervals of the day:
the third, the sixth, the ninth;
which we may find in the Scriptures
to have been more solemn than the rest.

179

The first infusion of the Holy Spirit
into the congregated disciples
took place at 'the third hour.'

Peter, on the day during which he
experienced the vision of
Universal Community,
exhibited in that small vessel;
had ascended into
the more lofty parts of the house,
for prayer's sake, 'at the sixth hour.'

The same Apostle was going into the Temple,
with John, 'at the ninth hour,'
when he restored the paralytic to health.

These practices stand simply,
without any precept for their observance.

Still, it may be granted a good thing
to establish some definite presumption;
which may both add stringency
to the admonition to pray,
and may, as though it were by a law;
tear us out from our businesses,
to such a duty.

What we read to have been
observed by Daniel also
(in accordance, of course,
with Israel's discipline);
we pray at least not less than
three times in the day,
debtors as we are to Three:
Father, Son, and Holy Spirit.

Of course, in addition to our
regular prayers; which are due,
without any admonition,
on the entrance of
light and night.

It is becoming to believers not to take food,
and not to go to the baths,
before interposing
a prayer.

For the refreshments
and nourishments of the spirit
are to be held prior to those of the flesh,
and things heavenly prior to
things earthly."

200's A.D. - The Early Church

The Early Church during persecution held worship services in underground tombs: the Catacombs. They added to the three traditional prayer times of the Jewish people, observed by the Apostles in the Book of Acts, by simply continuing to pray every three hours.

Following the time of the New Testament, the observance of The Threefold Daily Prayers that we find recorded there were included as three of the seven Canonical Hours of Prayer, or Divine Office.

The word *Office* was derived from *"official* times of prayer."

They have been observed continuously for the past two thousand years, in both the Eastern Orthodox and Roman Catholic Communions; by monastics, clergy, and those especially dedicated.

New Testament

With the freedom that we have in Christ, God does nowhere *require* their observance, but did God *sanction* the three times of prayer at 9 a.m., Noon, and 3 p.m.?

That is, did He *"ratify, confirm, and approve"* them?

Did God do this when He granted miracles, visions, and even the giving of the Holy Spirit for the birth of the Church at these *three specific* times, *while* the Apostles and other believers were *observing* these three times of prayer?

7.5 Sanctioned by God

"Every day has exactly 1,440 minutes;
can't you find even 10 of them
to be with your heavenly Father?

Doesn't God deserve
the best minutes
of your day?"

-Billy Graham (1918-2018)

Not *Commanded* by God, but *Sanctioned* by Him

Webster's Dictionary defines the word *sanction* as:

"To give sanction to;
to ratify; to confirm;
to approve."

We know that God desires us to *"Pray without ceasing."* (1 Thessalonians 5:17). But why would you want to pray at certain particular times? You may in fact already be doing so.

A common practice for most Christians is offering prayer three times a day, before meals. We thank God for His gift to us of our food. G*racias* in Spanish, and *grazie* in Italian, both mean *thank you*.

In English, we give thanks to God by *saying grace*.

Christ Sanctions *Saying Grace* by His Example

In the New Testament we see our Lord offering prayer before meals. He neither instructed nor commanded us to do this: to *"say grace."*

Like The Threefold Daily Prayers, this was a Jewish *custom*.

Saying grace before meals is not a part of the Law of Moses, and its observance is neither commanded nor required anywhere in the Bible.

However, Christ *sanctioned* the practice of *"saying grace"* before meals *by observing it Himself* when feeding the multitudes, and also when instituting the Last Supper:

"He took the seven loaves and the fish,
and gave thanks,
and broke them, and gave them to
His disciples, and the disciples
gave them to the multitude."

-Matthew 15:36

———

"When He had so spoken,
He took bread,
and gave thanks to God
in the presence of them all.
And when He had broken it,
He began to eat."

-Acts 27:35

———

"...the Lord Jesus, the same night
in which he was betrayed,
took bread; and when He
had given thanks,
He broke it, and said:

'Take, eat: this is My body,
which is given for you.
Do this, in remembrance of Me.'"

-1 Corinthians 11:24

———

"And He took the cup, and gave thanks,
and gave it to them, saying:
'Drink from it, all of you;
for this is My blood
of the New Covenant,
which is shed for the many,
for the forgiveness of sins."

-Matthew 26:27-28

Sanctioned in Paul's Letter to Timothy

We find an additional and even more strongly implied *sanction* for our practice of *"saying grace"* before meals, in the first letter of Paul to Timothy:

"...certain foods,
which God has created
to be received with
thanksgiving,
by those who believe
and know the truth.

Every creation of God is good,
and nothing is to be rejected,
if it is received
with thanksgiving.

For it is sanctified
by the word of God
and prayer.

If you instruct
the brothers and sisters
to remember these things,
you shall be a good minister of Christ,
nourished by the words of faith,
and of good teaching."

-1 Timothy 4:3-6

Sanctioned by God Seven Times In the New Testament

It could have taken place at any time of day or night:

But God chose to send the Holy Spirit for the birth of the Church on the *Day of Pentecost* at the time of the **Morning Prayer (9 a.m.: the Third Hour):**

"For these are not drunk,
as you suppose; seeing that
*it is only **nine in the morning."***

-Acts 2:15

184

S.G. Preston

It could have taken place at any time of day or night:

But God chose to give Peter a vision that would result in the acceptance of Gentiles into the Church at the time of the **Noon Prayer (the Sixth Hour):**

"On the next day
they went on their journey.
As they drew near to the city, Peter went up on the housetop
to pray, at about the noon hour.

He became very hungry, and would have eaten;
but while they made everything ready,
he fell into a trance..."

-Acts 10:9

It could have taken place at any time of day or night:

But God chose the time of the **Evening Prayer (3 p.m.: the Ninth Hour)** to send an angel to the Centurion Cornelius:

"There was a certain man in Caesarea called Cornelius;
a Centurion of the regiment called the Italian Cohort.

He was a devout man,
one that reverenced God with all his household.
He gave much charity to the people, and prayed to God always.

*In **a vision** he saw distinctly,*
at about three in the afternoon,
an angel of God coming to him and saying, 'Cornelius.'"

-Acts 10:1-3

———

"And Cornelius said, "Four days ago,
I was fasting until this same time;
three in the afternoon;
***when I began praying** in my house.*

Suddenly a man stood before me in bright clothing..."

-Acts 10:30

185

It could have taken place at any time of day or night:

But God chose the time of the **Evening Prayer (3 pm: the Ninth Hour)** for the miracle of the healing of the lame man, through Peter and John:

"Now Peter and John
went up together
into the Temple
at the hour of prayer,
being three in the afternoon.

And a certain man,
lame from his mother's womb,
was carried,
who they lay daily
at the Gate of the Temple
which is called Beautiful,
to ask for coins from those
who entered into
the Temple.

He, seeing Peter and John about to
go into the Temple,
asked for coins.

Peter and John looking at him,
said, 'Look at us.'

The lame man looked at them,
expecting to receive something
from them.

Then Peter said,
'Silver and gold have I none,
but such as I have,
I give you:

In the name of
Jesus Christ of Nazareth,
rise up and walk."

-Acts 3:1-6

Recorded Examples for Our Instruction

Did God even *further sanction* these three special times of prayer?

That is, did He *ratify*; *confirm,* and *approve* them, by the very act of *recording* all of these things through the Holy Spirit in the New Testament itself?

"For everything written
in the Scriptures
was written to be examples
for our instruction…"

-Romans 15:4
1 Corinthians 10:11

Let us now look at one final section of Holy Scripture. One which is so essential to our faith:

The Crucifixion of our Lord.

7.6 The Crucifixion & The Threefold Daily Prayers

"Eucastrophe (eu-cas-tro-phe):
A sudden and favourable resolution
of events in a story; a happy ending."

-Oxford English Dictionary

——

"The birth of Christ is the
eucastrophe of Man's history.

The Resurrection is the eucastrophe
of the story of the Incarnation.

This story begins and ends in joy.

It has pre-eminently
the 'inner consistency of reality.'

There is no tale ever told
that men would rather find was true,
and none which so many skeptical men
have accepted as true on its own merits.

For the Art of it has the supremely
convincing tone of Primary Art,
that is, of Creation.

To reject it leads either
to sadness or to wrath."

-J.R.R. Tolkien (1892-1973)

——

"Mor I an fhirrinne,
agus buaidhfe si."

"Truth is great
and will prevail."

-Old Gaelic Saying

S.G. Preston

9 a.m. (The Third Hour): Christ Is Crucified for Us
Noon (The Sixth Hour): Darkness Over the Whole Land Until...
3 p.m. (The Ninth Hour): Our Lord Gives Up His Spirit

Every morning at 9 a.m., a Lamb was sacrificed in the Temple. Christ was Crucified at 9 a.m., the exact time of the Morning Sacrifice (and therefore also of the Morning Prayer) in fulfillment of Christ's being:

> *"...the Lamb of God, who takes*
> *away the sins of the world."*

> -John 1:29

(Boldface mine):

> ***"It was nine in the morning,***
> *and they crucified Him.*
>
> *The inscription of His accusation*
> *was written above:*
>
> *THE KING OF THE JEWS."*
>
> -Mark 15:25-26

> ***"When the noon hour had arrived,***
> *there was darkness over the whole land*
> *until **three in the afternoon.***
>
> -Mark 15:33

> ***At three in the afternoon,***
> *Jesus cried out with a loud voice,*
> *saying, 'Eloi, Eloi, lama sabachthani?'*
> *which is, being interpreted,*
> *'My God, My God,*
> *why have You forsaken Me?"*
>
> *And some of those that stood by, when they heard it,*
> *said, 'See, He calls Elijah.'*

189

One of them ran
and filled a sponge full of vinegar,
and put it on a reed,
and gave Him it to drink from, saying,
'Leave Him alone.

Let us see whether Elijah
will arrive and take Him down.'

Jesus cried out with a loud voice,
and gave up the spirit.

The veil of the Temple was torn in two,
from the top to the bottom."

-Mark 15:34-38

In Remembrance

The Apostle Paul instructed us concerning our observance of Communion:

"For as often as you eat this bread,
and drink this cup,
you proclaim the Lord's death
until His return."

-1 Corinthians 11:26

The observance of *The Threefold Daily Prayers*; the three special hours of prayer of:

"...the third, the sixth, the ninth;
which we may find in the Scriptures to
have been more solemn than the rest."

...serve as a reminder to us of *our Lord's ultimate sacrifice of Himself on our behalf.*

One that is brought to mind at least *three times* each day.

* * *

190

Christ Our Intercessor

"Cast all your cares upon Him, for He cares for you." -1 Peter 5:7

"Having therefore boldness to enter into the Holy of Holies by the blood of Jesus:" (Hebrews 10:19)

"Let us then go boldly to the throne of grace, so that we can receive mercy, and find grace to help in time of need." -Hebrews 4:16

———

"For Christ has not entered into the holy places made with hands, which are only copies of the true one; but into heaven itself; now to appear in the presence of God for us..." -Hebrews 9:24

"Therefore He is able to save to the uttermost those that draw near to God through Him, seeing He ever lives to make intercession for them." -Hebrews 7:25

———

"I pray for them: I do not pray for the world, but for those that You have given to Me, for they are Yours." -John 17:9

"I do not pray that You should take them out of the world, but that You should keep them from the evil." -John 17:15

———

"My little children, these things I write to you, so that you do not sin. But if anyone sins, we have an advocate with the Father, Jesus Christ the righteous: He is the propitiation for our sins; and not for ours only, but also for the sins of the whole world." -1 John 2:2

"Who is he that that condemns? It is Christ that died, yes rather, that is risen, who is even at the right hand of God, who also makes intercession for us." -Romans 8:34

"If God is for us, who can be against us?" -Romans 8:31

* * *

St. Basil the Great (329-379 A.D.)

*"When you sit down to eat, pray. When you eat bread,
do so thanking Him for being so generous to you.*

*...When you dress, thank Him for His kindness
in providing you with clothes.*

*When you look at the sky and the beauty of the stars,
throw yourself at God's feet and adore Him
who in His wisdom has arranged things in this way.*

*Similarly, when the sun goes down and when it rises,
when you are asleep or awake, give thanks to God,
who created and arranged all things for your benefit,
to have you know, love and praise your Creator."*

———

*"Troubles are usually the brooms and shovels
that smooth the road to a good man's fortune;
and many a man curses the rain that falls upon his head,
and knows not that it brings abundance
to drive away hunger."*

———

"As we were baptized, so we profess our belief.

As we profess our belief, so also, we offer praise.

*As then baptism has been given us by the Savior,
in the name of the Father and of the Son and of the Holy Spirit,
so, in accordance with our baptism,
we make the confession of the creed..."*

———

*"A psalm implies serenity of soul; it is the author of peace,
which calms bewildering and seething thoughts.*

*For it softens the wrath of the soul,
and what is unbridled it chastens."*

* * *

S.G. Preston

Answers to Prayer
PrayerFoundation ™ 24-Hr. Prayerchain

June 17, 2002 - Answer to Prayer:

I had requested prayer for my financial situation and for my son who had a drug problem, and also is facing a trial for burglaries. My financial situation is *much* improved. Thank you so much for your prayers.

I thought the only solution would be to win the lottery or something. However, God had other plans.

My husband had been paying a huge amount of support to his ex-wife. She took him to Court for more. The Judge decided in his favor, and he doesn't have to pay any anymore. This is incredible and certainly an answer to prayers. Now we have enough money to pay the bills! Also, my son is doing well, and is now off drugs.

Thank you so very much for your prayers.

-Mom in Pennsylvania

Answer to Prayer Update - Aug. 8, 2002

You have been praying for my son.

He was addicted to heroin, lost his house and good job, and was falsely accused by his girlfriend (when she was caught) of house robberies that *she* had committed.

He is now working hard, and has not used drugs for six months.

Thank you so much,

-Mom in Pennsylvania

(From the book: *Answers to Prayer* by S.G. Preston)

8. *Prayer Leads to Evangelism*

8.1 Brother Paul in the U.K.

"O give thanks to the Lord; call upon His Name:
make known His deeds among the people."

-Psalm 105:1

———

"The Celtic Church was strongest in the three areas
I think most of us would admit are the most needful,
and in which we are the most neglectful:

Prayer, Bible Study, and Evangelism.

Heaven knows we need to be more than conquerors
through Christ in these."

-Paul D.J. Arblaster
From his book, *Celtic Christianity:*
Yesterday, Today, and for the Future

Directing Steve McQueen

Paul D.J. Arblaster was born in Bloxwich, England.

A graduate of the London Film School, he also holds a B.A. from the University of Oregon.

Besides being involved in the international antiques trade and teaching for many years, he has produced numerous documentaries throughout his career.

In the early 1980's, he founded an international Christian Motorcycle group, and directed Steve McQueen in *Full Throttle to Glory,* which was voted among the top ten documentaries on Public Access Television.

Apart from classic motorcycles and Celtic Christianity, his interests include maritime lore, antiques, history, and walking ancient pathways with his American wife, Carol. They have three children.

194

S.G. Preston

Called to Evangelism

Brother Paul is also the Founder of the *Celtic Evangelism Fellowship* (CEF). In 2002 his first book, *Celtic Christianity Yesterday, Today, and for the Future: Gleaning Wisdom from the Primitive Protestants* was published.

In 2003 Paul became a member of the *PrayerFoundation Knights of Prayer*.™

In 2004, he and Carol went into full-time Evangelism in England with *Cutting Edge Ministries,* providing Evangelism Support for Local Churches. CEM is an interdenominational ministry; a member of the Evangelical Alliance.

King Arthur and the Island of Avalon

Glastonbury Tor (Hill) is associated with stories of King Arthur.

Standing alone atop the Tor is St. Michael's Tower, the ruins of what remains of what was once a Church and Monastery. Inhabited since the Iron Age, Glastonbury Tor is said to be the location of the first Church and Monastery in England.

Before that it was the location of a famous pagan site. In very ancient pagan times the hill was surrounded by a lake, making it an island known as *Avalon.*

Glastonbury Festival

Because of this history, today Glastonbury Tor is the site of the annual *Glastonbury Festival.*

Concerts are provided by leading Rock and Pop Bands; as well as dance, comedy, theatre, circus, cabaret and other performing arts. It has an annual attendance of 200,000 people.

Carol is an excellent Harpist who has recorded several music CDs. She played her harp in a booth at this festival for many years, while Paul talked to the onlookers about Jesus.

Brother Paul has also had a Chaplaincy at the 13th Century St. Mary Magdalene Church in the town of Glastonbury.

———

Your Comments (10/17/03):

I met Paul and Carol at a Celtic Festival in Elizabethton, Tennessee a little over a year ago.

I was attracted to their booth by Carol's beautiful harp playing, and struck up a conversation with Paul about *Celtic Christianity*.

I was born again in 1963 in Hampton, Virginia and as I've matured in my faith, I've really developed an appreciation for the devotion and personal witness that was so evident in the lives of the early Celtic Saints.

As I've explored my Celtic roots, I've become especially appreciative of the lives of men like *Saint Patrick* and *Saint Columba*.

The values of *Celtic Christianity* that Paul talked about really fit into place with what the Lord was already doing in my heart, and it has really made a difference in my life.

My personal prayer life and witnessing have taken on renewed meaning, and I'm experiencing a deeper sense of joy and peace.

I'm working through your curriculum, and participating in your *24-Hr. Prayerchain* ministry each morning between 4:00 and 4:30 Eastern Time. I really enjoy getting up early before the day gets too far ahead of me.

The materials on your website have been really helpful. Thank you so much.

I'm happy to hear that Paul and Carol have been working in England.

I bought a copy of *Celtic Christianity: Yesterday, Today, and for the Future* when I met Paul, and he signed it:

> *"Hear ye the Word of the Lord, O ye nations,*
> *and declare it unto the isles afar off..."*

-Jeremiah 31:10

It sounds like he's taken that verse personally to heart.

Wishing you the Peace of God and His Richest Blessings,

-Tom C. (Maryland)

S.G. Preston

Monastery Visitors

For three Christmas seasons we were blessed to be able to meet with Brother Paul and his wife Carol here in Vancouver, Washington.

They were visiting from England, where they were serving as Missionaries in their full-time Christian evangelism ministry.

Paul took the beautiful photo of Lindisfarne at the top of our webpage: *Aidan's Prayer* (*Lindisfarne*), under the *Prayer Category* in the dropdown Menu. We invite all who read this page to support them with your prayers.

Also please pray for Lay Monk Denise, who teaches Missionaries' children in Japan, and who visited us from there with her daughter.

Later, she wrote us that when they had visited a church using incense in their service, her daughter said to her:

"It smells like the Monks' house."

Excerpted From the Book:

Celtic Christianity Yesterday, Today, and for the Future:
Gleaning Wisdom from the Primitive Protestants
by Paul D.J. Arblaster

More Dangerous than Viking Raiders -- Our Modern Culture

I am not putting forth Celtic Christianity as some panacea of perfection; it is a process and a tool for overcoming that which may be more dangerous than Viking raiders -- our modern culture.

It must be admitted that not all aspects of Celtic Christianity could, or even should, be followed today, but it does offer much we may appropriate as an arsenal to combat the cultural seduction of our time and affections.

The Celtic Church was strongest in the three areas I think most of us would admit are the most needful, and in which we are the most neglectful: Prayer, Bible Study, and Evangelism.

Heaven knows we need to be more than conquerors through Christ in these.

197

Celtic Missionary Saints

When Celtic missionary saints stepped into boats to allow the wind and currents to guide them wherever God willed, they basically put everything on the line and turned their back on comfortable predictability. In a sense they became dead to this world.

Christ told us to be willing to risk no less, for ultimately he promised us no loss compared to what we would gain. We today can take as bold a step without ever leaving our locality; call it the prayer of death ("For me to live is Christ, to die is gain.").

An old adage is, "Be careful what you pray for, God might just grant it!" We all have things we enjoy spending a lot of time and energy on that could more profitably be spent in eternal things.

It takes a lot of courage to ask God completely to re-orient us, away from our cultural fixations, and into His value system instead. If you are willing to have God start this process, it can begin with a very simple, yet dangerous prayer, "Lord, let me lose interest in all temporal diversions."

Conversation with the Father

If you begin in truth with this step of faith, your life can become every bit as adventurous as the Celtic Saints experiencing God working through them. In our regular prayers we are often guilty of rushing through into specific requests of God with what is a cursory, but perhaps not very deeply felt, introductory acknowledgement of thanks to Him for His greatness.

Tozer's classic, *The Knowledge of the Holy*, along with Keller's *A Shepherd looks at The Lord's Prayer/Psalm 23* should be read and read again, because one has a tendency to forget the magnitude and anticipation of joy attendant with entering into conversation with the Father through the Son by the Holy Spirit.

While He is so high above us, He is also all around us and in us. Dwelling on this great mystery alone is enough to evoke feelings of awe.

S.G. Preston

Comments From Brother Paul:

I just got back from Gloucester at CEM (*Cutting Edge Ministries*) HQ and found your letter there along with Brother Danny's CD. We know people into soft and creative jazz will find it well done.

I don't know what stock you put into blessings these days by those not of the official cloth, but a blessing be upon you, and the Foundation you founded. We hope to be in touch so we can arrange to get together with you whilst we are in Oregon.

Love in Christ; we do appreciate you both,

Paul and Carol Arblaster (U.K.)

Note: We love Brother Paul and Carol. Their dedication to God in their ministry of Evangelism has been a great inspiration to us. Paul was among the earliest to became a Brother in our Order, and both of them then later left the U.S. to share the Gospel as full-time Missionaries in England.

8.2 Lay Monk Danny: God's Musician

"Sing to Him a new song;
play skillfully with a loud noise."

-Psalm 33:3

———

"Begin now to be
what you will be hereafter."

-St. Jerome (347-420 A.D.)

Becoming a Lay Monk and Releasing a Music CD

In 1999 when Lay Monk Linda and I were led to co-found the *PrayerFoundation*,™ there were two other original members:

One was Lay Monk Bob, and the other was Lay Monk Danny: a young African-American Jazz musician.

That same year, Danny released a Music CD that he had Produced himself with his own recording equipment, and on which he had played every instrument, including guitar and keyboards.

Two years later, in 2001, a local radio station had his CD, *"Take It Easy,"* reviewed by Becky Harrison for their Music Guide Magazine. In the same issue, they commissioned a second article on Danny by writer Patti David.

Both writers were kind enough to grant me permission to re-print their articles, which I have included here:

New Treatment for Brain Problem Available

By Patti David

Debilitating Headaches, Blindness, and Paralysis

Portland guitarist Danny Drayer had been suffering from debilitating headaches for a long time.

When he would see Doctors, the diagnosis was that he had the flu.

200

AVMs

No one knew how serious the condition really was, until the headaches that Danny was having began causing blindness, and paralysis in his legs for a month at a time. Drayer has an abnormally large Arterial Venus Malformation, which affects six out of every 1,000 people.

"One percent of all strokes are caused by or associated with AVMs," said Martin Johnson M.D., Drayer's neurosurgeon. Johnson, who has performed about four AVM resections or removals every year for the past 22 years, said that AVMs are congenital. AVMs are groups of torturously-malformed blood vessels found in the brain's cerebral hemispheres.

Like aneurisms, they can rupture at any time. Aneurisms affect only arteries, but AVMs affect all three types of blood vessels in the brain (arteries, veins, and capillaries).

Over 30 Neurosurgeries

Treated Embolization is the insertion of tiny silastic spheres into specific blood vessels, to channel blood flow away from the AVM. The technique had only been done at the Barrow Neurological Institute in Phoenix, Arizona, at the University of California in San Diego, and at Stanford University.

Charles Kerber M.D., of La Mesa, California, had to fly to Portland four times over an eight-week period to embolize Drayer. To date, Danny has undergone surgery over thirty times in attempts to correct this problem.

Once he was brought to the Hospital and declared DOA (Dead On Arrival). When he came back to life and learned of what had happened, Danny gave his life to Jesus. Now he gives thanks to God for every new day he receives.

"I'm a little scared, but I'm putting my faith in God.

You have to live out your life and live it to the fullest and be happy. I could be scheduled for surgery, but I could just as easily be hit by a truck, and it would be my time to go. So I'm not living on thin ice, I'm just being happy."

CD: *"Take It Easy"* by Danny L. Drayer...

By Becky Harrison

If you fancy meaningful harmony on guitar, drums, and synthesizer, check out Danny Drayer, a brilliant musician and composer who created his CD: *"Take It Easy."* Not letting anything hold him back, Danny produced, designed, composed, arranged, and played every instrument on his own musical release.

"I couldn't postpone my musical dream anymore."

The quality of *"Take It Easy"* is very smooth and sounds as though it were mixed in a large studio. All ten tracks are wonderfully mixed and pleasant to the ears.

"Wings, track number eight, is dedicated to my late brother, Victor, and my late sister, Beveline."

Danny has been a self-taught musician since the age of seven. He has survived an embolism and years of recovery, and never strayed from his passion. You can enjoy his music on *"Take It Easy.* (This Radio Station) has a copy in (its) music library; you can call and request a few tracks from Danny's CD.

Once your ears have fallen in love with the music, you can call and request your own copy.

———

(2020) Comments from Lay Monk William

To Lay Monk Danny & All My Brother and Sister *Knights of Prayer Lay Monks* ™ Throughout the World:

My brothers and sisters in China are under the gun, strong, and growing. Glory be to our Father and His Son Jesus Christ. I am planning a trip to Uganda next winter, Lord willing. I will be working with two orphanages there, being grandfather, storyteller, and helping students write letters to sponsors here in the USA and in Europe.

Your prayers and thoughts are like gold.

-Lay Monk William (Missionary)

S.G. Preston

Hudson Taylor On Prayer, Missions, & Christ

"When I get to China,
I will have no claim on anyone for anything.
My claim will be in God alone,
and I must learn before I leave England
to move men through God by prayer alone."

"All God's giants have been weak men and women
who have gotten hold of God's faithfulness."

———

"...I cannot describe how I long to be a missionary;
to carry the Glad Tidings to poor, perishing sinners;
to spend and be spent for Him who died for me!
...Think...of twelve millions --
a number so great that it is impossible to realize it --
yes, twelve million souls in China, every year,
passing without God and without hope
into eternity...

Oh let us look with compassion on this multitude!
God has been compassionate with us;
let us be like Him..."

———

"Carrying the cross does mean following in Jesus' footsteps.
And in His footsteps are rejection, brokenheartedness,
persecution and death.

There are not two Christs -
an easygoing one for easygoing Christians,
and a suffering one for exceptional believers.

There is only one Christ."
Are we willing to follow
His lead?"

-Hudson Taylor (1832-1905)
Founder: *China Inland Mission*

* * *

203

8.3 *Dear Celtic Lay Monks*

Glaodh àrd, is urnuigh ni mi ris, moch, feasgar, s meadhon-là,
Is eisdidh e gu grad ri m ghlaodh."

"Evening, and morning, and at noon: I will pray,
and call out loud; and He shall hear my voice."

-Psalm 55:17 in Gaelic

I found your Site and I am enjoying your articles. I am a pastor that has become involved in *Celtic Christianity*. We would appreciate your prayers, as we are doing a similar thing in South Florida. Blessings,

-Mike & Daryl, Ann Z.+ (Davie, Florida)

I found your prayer website, and although I have not completely gone through it, I am impressed with what the Lord has led you into. I was a minister for 30 years and have been led by the Lord into the *Anglican Mission in the Americas*.

It is part of the Anglican Communion worldwide, and is Bible believing and *evangelical*.

I was looking for a web site for *Daily Prayer* when I came across yours. I have always been impressed by *Celtic Christian* spirituality, especially as practiced by *Columba* and *Patrick*, etc. I will check out your web site more... Rejoicing with you in the Lord,

-Jim O.+

Dear *Knights of Prayer*, ™ Thank you so much for your prayers. Again, thank you so, so much. God bless you all.

-Sandra T. (Kuala Lumpur, Malaysia)

204

S.G. Preston

I Praise The Living LORD for finding your website! I was drawn to search out *Protestant Friars* **and I came upon your Site.** I love what you are doing and I have been so refreshed and inspired - and that's not easy for us unemotional Brits.

Always been fascinated by the life of a contemplative. I visited a Franciscan Friary in Alnmouth (near Holy Island...Lindisfarne).

What I have lacked in my life is the routine of prayer that belonging to an "Order" can bring.

I was a Youth Pastor (for about 6 years) as well as Youth Leader, and part of the Church "oversight." I was the children's Sunday School teacher as well as the Bible Teacher for our Church.

I have already read some of your *Recommended Books*. I wish there were things on your web-site I could disagree with, because it all appears too good to be true. It is almost as if *I* had written the website!

Although I have not visited *Lindisfarne*, I have stayed on *Iona* in Scotland. A beautiful and almost mysterious Island of peace and tranquility. I can understand why the Celtic Fathers chose that place.

In regards to *Francis*, he has been a hero of mine and found something I would love to experience. His love of all things, even nature, and his adoration of our Lord is an inspiration to all.

-Gaz M. (U.K.)

Dear friends in Jesus, Greetings from New Zealand. In your Statement of Faith you say, and rightly so, that the Bible is the Word of God. New Zealand has many prayer warriors like yourselves.

The first settlers and the later immigrants have a record of evangelism that echoes that of the Celtic saints.

Please pray for Israel. God bless you, fellow travelers.

-Madeleine (New Zealand)

Dear Friends, a question was running through my mind as to whether or not there were any lay monasteries in existence. I had contemplated speaking to others about forming one, when I decided to check first on the Internet.

And there your Site appeared! What a wonderful revelation! I want to thank God for you and those of you who have made this a reality. Perhaps someday I will be able to visit you and learn more.

In the meantime, I just wanted you to know that I believe you are part of a movement in the Church that will have long lasting effects in the lives of people. Blessings,

-Raph M.

(Survey)
Liked Best? **Your existence and commitment.**
Born Again? Yes.
Comments? Fountain in the desert; unbelievable.

-(Puerto Rico)

I am a Free Lutheran Pastor in Nebraska and I have thoroughly enjoyed going through your website. I am prayerfully considering becoming a member of your Order. May God richly bless you in your work in His kingdom.

Please pray for our congregation and keep me on your Newsletter emailing list. Blessings,

-Pastor David W. (Nebraska)

Thank you for your Site and direction.
-Kathleen D. (Ireland)

Dear Lay Monk Preston, thank you so much, and glory to God. I know these chapters and have read them so many times and found no solace. It is a wonder how sometimes you can read chapters and not see anything but the words.

I have sat down in the quiet of my lounge this morning and read your email again, with the scriptures, and I can clearly see what God is trying to tell me. Thank you so much, and I will visit your webpages. Yours in Christ,

-Robert R.

My name is Hans and I work with *Youth With A Mission* in Stockholm, Sweden. I am involved in our Discipleship Schools and teach especially on missions.

For years I have been looking for a movie/documentary on the *Moravian movement* and *Count Zinzendorf.* I saw on your website that you are having this documentary...I hope you can help me out. In His love for the unreached,

-Hans and Jeanet, *Youth With A Mission* (Stockholm, Sweden)

I am very intrigued by your website. I have considered myself a Celtic Christian and an emerging prayer warrior. My deep desire is to see radical change in lives by the power of prayer and to pray for the Lord's return.

I am very attracted to a monastic lifestyle that can blend with my family responsibilities...

Your *PrayerFoundation* ™ is exactly what I have looked for, for a long time, but I see the level of commitment (reading, prayer and Scripture study), and realize that saying yes to this means saying no to a thousand other things. Blessings,

-Susanne H. (Switzerland)

Greetings, My Beloved Brother And Sister In Christ! My life has completely changed by following the information and requirements on the *PrayerFoundation* ™ website since over a year and a half ago.

I love Jesus Christ, and I love you and pray for you and others -- always. I have met the requirements thus far on my journey and wish to grow closer to God with each day.

I have actually never been happier, and this I owe to you Lay Monk Linda, and to you Lay Monk Preston. My life is full.

I love your updated website, and if you could, please send a new *Monastic Certificate and Card* (I know how busy you are!).

May God Continue To Bless Your Work,

-Lay Monk Elli (Colorado)

I am so glad I happened onto your Site. I am very interested in my Irish Heritage and in personal evangelism. Here, I find them combined.

Thank you, you have obviously put a great deal of work into your website, it is so full of interesting things.

-Gregg C. (Texarkana, Texas)

(Survey)
Liked Best? **That you taught me to Pray the Hours and the wonderful suggestions to deepen my relationship with Our Lord.**
I want *More!* ^-^
Born-again? Yes.
Visit Site? Daily.
Comments? Extremely informative and easy to navigate as well as friendly in appearance. Keep up the good work.

-(England)

S.G. Preston

Greetings in the wonderful name of our Sweet Saviour Jesus Christ. I am so impressed by your ministry. In fact, every day I see it. I feel it is an answer to my prayer. I always wanted to become a lay monk. I am married and living in India... I really want to experience, as I truly believe every born again Christian has to be consecrated, whether laity or religious. God bless you,

-Anuradha R. (India)

I am contemplating becoming a Lay monk... Thank you.

-Aidan B. (Dublin, Ireland)

I'm a minister in the Cumberland Presbyterian Church, who are proud of their *Celtic* heritage. I have been much in the Nazarene Church, my wife's heritage and much blessed by this association.

Please put me on your monthly E-Newsletter list and the Intercessor-*Prayer Warrior* list. I am enjoying reading page after page of your website.

-John (Tennessee)

Dear Friends, Thank you for your email Newsletter. Message is wonderful.

-Jesuratnam (India)

Hooray for Lay Monk Bob! What a courageous man of God. Thanks for profiling him.

-Lay Monk Christine (Hawaii)

8.4 Lay Monk Bob & the Falling Stars

"...and the stars shall fall from heaven...
...and they shall see the Son of Man
arriving in the clouds of heaven
with power and great glory."

-Matthew 24:29,30

Tent Meeting

Lay Monk Bob served with the U.S. Navy in the Pacific during World War II. Later in life, he served for years on the Board of Directors of a local Bible-believing Church in Portland, Oregon and many more years on the Board of Directors of the *PrayerFoundation.*™

But at one time, he was a very young man, and still a new Christian...

Having received Christ when he was nineteen through reading the New Testament, Lay Monk Bob soon felt led to go out frequently and preach the good news that Jesus saves. He shared the gospel of our Savior in the city streets throughout different parts of the nation.

Now, an unusual event occurred. After being saved only for a few months, Bob attended the tent meeting of Joe Hankins for three weeks. Joe, a marvelous preacher, not only preached on the Cross, but also frequently talked about the *very soon* return of Christ.

Joe's preaching so stirred Lay Monk Bob that he took very literally Matthew 24:27, which says:

"For as the lightning arrives from the east,
and shines even to the west;
so also shall be the arrival of the Son of Man."

One Night in the Hospital

In Lay Monk Bob's own words: *"Believing then that Jesus would come in the sky out of the east, so to the east I looked.*

I began each morning and evening to set my eyes to the eastern sky expecting perhaps today He will come; then concluding, 'Not today.'"

210

S.G. Preston

The Stars Are Falling

About that time, one night in the Hospital where the Navy had sent me to recover (from an arm injury), I was reading the Bible to a fellow sailor, including the verses, Mark 13:25-26 which state:

> *"And the stars of heaven shall fall, and the powers that are in heaven shall be shaken.*
>
> *Then shall they see the Son of Man arriving in the clouds with great power and glory.*
>
> *And then shall He send His angels, and shall gather together His elect from the four winds; from the farthest parts of the earth to the farthest part of heaven."*

At the exact moment when I had finished reading those verses, someone ran in from outside shouting loudly:

"Look! The stars are falling The stars are falling!" I and my friend (who was not a Christian) ran quickly outside and looked up into the night sky.

Everywhere by the hundreds, stars were falling. The year was 1946. This also happened in November of 2002, when 6,000 *"falling stars"* (meteorites) could be seen falling each hour. As I looked up, my hair stood straight up. I grabbed the sailor's hand and lifted our hands up toward heaven, shouting, *"This is it! He's returning!"*

I Wanted You to Know This...

Five years passed. Both of us were out of the Service and had parted our ways. One day as I returned home, I opened the door, and there stood the same young man. How he had found me, I don't know.

He said, *"Remember when you read the scriptures, and we ran outside and looked up and said "This is it! He's returning!" and the stars were falling everywhere...*

Well, I never had been saved before, but at that exact moment I gave my life to Jesus, and was saved.

I wanted you to know this."

211

8.5 Lay Monk Bob: Street Preacher of God

*"A man becomes a Christian,
he is not born one."*

-Tertullian
(c. 150/160-After 220 A.D.)

———

*"Evangelism is just
one beggar
telling another beggar
where to find bread."*

-D.T. Niles (1908-1970)
Evangelist, Pastor
President: *Ceylon Methodist Conference*

Bear One Another's Burdens (Galatians 6:2)

We receive over 300 emails every day, sent to *PrayerFoundation Lay Monks* ™ from all over the world.

Many are heart-breaking, and cause us to re-examine our own Christian lives.

*"Honor Christ
as Lord in your heart,*

*and always be ready
to give an answer
to anyone
who asks you,*

*a reason for the hope
that is in you."*

-1 Peter 3:15

Some of those who have Registered and become Lay Monks with our Monastic Order have traveled to other continents as full-time missionaries. Some of us here, too.

S.G. Preston

Lay Monk Bob in Portland

"Buinidh urram do'n aois."

"Honor belongs to old age."

-Old Gaelic Saying

Three times a day, Monday through Friday, and twice on Saturday; for about an hour each time...for the twenty-five or so years following his retirement, Lay Monk Bob could be found telling others about Jesus on the busy streets of downtown Portland, Oregon.

Bob has sometimes been joined by other Christians in his ministry. Some of these street-preached or did one-on-one witnessing, while others passed out Gospel tracts. That is, except when Bob was away preaching the Good News of Christ in Mexico.

Missionary Journeys to Mexico

Fluent in Spanish, Lay Monk Bob traveled to Mexico 42 times to share the Gospel there.

He paid for these trips himself, and for the many Bible tracts that he handed to people in Portland and in Mexico, out of his own meager Social Security income. He would always take the bus to keep his costs down.

In Mexico, the police are often soldiers in the army. The country is divided into 31 States. Some States allow preaching of the Gospel on the streets, and some do not.

A Soldier With a Shotgun

On one of his missionary journeys, Bob got off the bus, unaware that he had arrived in a part of Mexico where the authorities do not allow anyone to preach Christ on the streets, or even hand out Gospel tracts.

Lay Monk Bob began telling people about Jesus' love for them.

A soldier walked up to Bob, who was then in his eighties, pointed the barrel of a shotgun at Bob's head, and ordered him to leave that State immediately.

Living On Faith

At some point in time; and I don't actually know for how many years he was doing this, for I learned about it accidentally; Bob was "living on faith."

He was *praying in* all of the money he used to pay his rent and buy the few things that he needed, and giving out *all* of his meager Social Security income to those who, as he said:

"Needed it more."

Persecution

Verbal abuse and shouted obscenities were a daily occurrence, as were threats of violence.

He had boiling coffee thrown on him many times.

One man who threw coffee on Bob returned a few days later to do it again. Several days later he sat down beside Monk Bob and apologized.

A Great Joy

This man continued visiting and sitting near Bob; now attentive to, and thankful for, God's Word. He received Christ; becoming a Christian through Lay Monk Bob's ministry.

The man joined a Church, and two years later, met and married a Christian woman. Three years later, he walked over to show Bob a picture of his new four-month old baby.

Bob said about this:

"There is a great joy...
the joy of meeting someone
you'd led to the Lord years before,
who is still strong
for Christ."

There were other unexpected joys, like when a man, hearing Lay Monk Bob's preaching, ran across the street towards Bob, dropped his bag, fell on his knees, and asked to be prayed with to receive Christ's salvation.

214

More Blessings

On another occasion, when Lay Monk Bob was preaching in downtown Portland, a man listening to him began crying. This man said that he had been on his way to commit suicide, but when he heard Bob talking about Jesus' love for him, he could no longer do it.

We all ask ourselves: can our *one solitary life* really make a difference in this world? The answer is: Yes. Someone who would have been *separated* from God for all eternity will now be *with* God for all eternity.

A woman once came up to Lay Monk Bob and said:

"You preach with such love to the people."

Bob said about that woman:

*"That's what you want to hear.
There's been fourteen or fifteen times when I've felt
God's love for the lost so strongly that I had to stop preaching
before I started crying."*

Linda once told me how when she was a little girl, Bob, her Father, would often take her and her brother and sister with him to hand out tracts and Bible verses.

Lay Monk Bob went home to be with the Lord in 2015. He was not quite eighty-nine years old. His seventy years of service for God began when he accepted Jesus Christ as his personal Lord and Savior, at the age of nineteen.

Street Preacher of God

As told in my book, *Prayer as a Total Lifestyle: Learning from the Greatest Lives of Prayer,* Lay Monk Bob (1926-2015) was buried with full honors in a National Military Cemetery. Upon his headstone, beneath a Celtic Cross and the dates of his Service in the Navy during World War II, we had engraved the words:

Street Preacher of God.

8.6 Communion with Christ

"Dear brethren, if we shut our ears to what Jesus tells us,
we shall never have power in prayer,
nor shall we enjoy intimate communion
with the Well-beloved."

-Charles Spurgeon (1834-1892)
English Baptist; *"The Prince of Preachers"*

———

"All we have to decide is what to
do with the time that is given us."

-J.R.R. Tolkien (1892-1973)
Roman Catholic; Author: *The Lord of the Rings*

Prayer and Christ

We have heard one of our favorite Bible teachers, Dr. J. Vernon McGee, say over the Radio airwaves many times:

"Christianity is not a religion. Christianity is a person...Christ;
and you either have received Him as your Lord and Savior,
or you haven't."

It follows then that the Christian life is not a mere collection of religious observances, but Christ living in us and through us, moment by moment, day by day, through the power of the Holy Spirit.

Prayer and the Apostles

"Disregard the study of God, and you sentence yourself to stumble
and blunder through life blindfolded, as it were,
with no sense of direction and no understanding
of what surrounds you.

This way you can waste your life and lose your soul."

-J.I. Packer (1926-2020)
Author: *Knowing God*

Prayer and Great Prayer Christians

God has revealed Himself through His Word, where we learn about God and His will for our lives.

Prayer is indeed the essence of the Christian life, for it is our communion with the Father, through Christ, by the Holy Spirit.

As Peter said, speaking for all of the Apostles:

> *"But we will devote ourselves continually to prayer,*
> *and to the ministry of the word."*

> -Acts 6:4

This is not a book of theories about prayer. It is all practical, working information learned from personal experience: our own, and that of many of *the Greatest Lives of Prayer* throughout history. For they:

> *"...being dead, yet speak."*

> -Hebrews 11:4

Prayer and Hudson Taylor

Hudson Taylor taught us that:

> *"Believing prayer will lead to whole-hearted action."*

———

> *"My work is a very peculiar* (unique) *one;*
> *in many respects it has,*
> *and can have, no precedent.*

> *It may be called an experiment;*
> *to a certain extent it is so.*

> *And by God's help it shall be,*
> *as it is being faithfully made."*

———

> *"The Apostolic plan was not to raise ways and means,*
> *but to go and do the work."*

217

Bringing Others to Christ

From the very beginning of our ministry, half of the visitors to our website have not been Christians.

This was completely unexpected, but has been a wonderful, God-given opportunity for us to be able to present the Gospel message of Christ's forgiveness and salvation to them.

It is the greatest of blessings when we receive an email that someone has become a Christian by receiving Christ through the information provided on our website.

Originally, we did not think that very many who weren't already Christians would be looking at a Christian website. Perhaps because our website was so different from the typical Christian website, we soon learned through a Survey we posted online, that *half* of the visitors to our Site said that they were *not born again*.

We have no idea if this will continue with the books we are now publishing, but we hope that it does.

I repeat here a portion of one of the emails we received, that I have already posted at the beginning of this book (although this one is from someone who *did* have an earlier knowledge of the Gospel):

"I found your website. It disarmed me…It had none of the expected traditional, canned, glossy, homogenized, mainstream Christian visuals that I could sneer at. It intrigued me.

Where were the modern Christian stereotypes that I could vent my disillusionment, frustration, and bitterness towards?

It was old, really old. I love old...
it was so old that it was new again.

Because the symbols of the "modern" church, with all its baggage, were missing, I could look, once again, at the word of God, the purposes of God, the love of God, without being tripped-up by my anger at the failings of the modern institution of the church, and man.

Your web site was foundationally sound. It was a rock. It gave me traction. It led me back to Scripture. It led me back to my first love.

It led me back to God."

218

Those of us who have already received Christ as our personal Lord and Savior need to be sure that we have learned and memorized enough of God's word to be able *to explain it to others when asked.*

We consider our webpage: *How to Receive Christ* to be *our most important webpage.* We placed a "link" to this page on all of the 1,400-plus webpages on both of our websites. Our prayer is:

"May many more who are not Christians,
be brought into the
knowledge of Christ.

May many more who are Christians,
be brought into a deeper prayer life;
into deeper communion
with Christ.

In Jesus' Name we pray. Amen."

One message is presented consistently throughout the entire Old and New Testaments. It is the *Gospel* message, the *Good News* about Jesus Christ.

God's Plan of Salvation is Receiving Christ

Our Sin Has Separated Us From God

"Your iniquities have made
a separation between you
and your God."

-Isaiah 59:2

Salvation is a Gift from God (You Cannot Earn It):

"For the wages of sin is death;
but the gift of God
is eternal life through
Jesus Christ our Lord."

-Romans 6:23

Salvation Is *Only* Through Christ

"Jesus said to him,
'I am the way, the truth, and the life;
no one comes to the Father, except through Me.'"

-John 14:6

Turn from Your Sins to Christ

"Repent therefore, and be converted,
that your sins may be blotted out."

-Acts 3:19

Believe in Christ and Confess Him as Lord

"That if you shall confess
with your mouth the Lord Jesus,
and believe in your heart
that God has raised Him from the dead,
you shall be saved.

For with the heart one
believes unto righteousness;
and with the mouth
confession is made
unto salvation."

-Romans 10:9-10

Christ Is Inviting You to Call Upon Him Right Now

"Behold,
I stand at the door, and knock:
if anyone hears My voice,
and opens the door,
I will come in to him,
and will dine with him,
and he with Me."

-Revelation 3:20

9. *A Celtic Lay Monk Prayer Lifestyle*

9.1 Poem of Monk Manchan of Offaly

"...where all men's sins
are washed away
by sanctifying grace.

...and I to sit
at times alone,
and pray in
every place."

-St. Manchan (d. 664 A.D.)

Manchan of Offaly was One of St. Patrick's Converts

Offaly is a County in Ireland.

In this poem, Manchan tells how he went off to be a hermit monk, but disciples gathered around him, and he found himself the leader (Abbot) of a small group of monks!

This is how Celtic monasteries often began in the time period of 500-1100 A.D.

Manchan's poem describes what these early type of monastic communities were like.

They were small in number, twelve monks being considered the right size.

When they reached eighteen members, six of the monks would leave to begin a new monastery.

Trinity College; Dublin, Ireland

We first read this poem in the Visitor's Center at Trinity College in Dublin, Ireland, where the *Book of Kells* is on display.

It is also found along with a wonderful stanza by stanza explanatory commentary in the book *How the Irish Saved Civilization* by Thomas Cahill.

St. Manchan of Offaly's Poem

Composed c. 450-550 A.D.

Grant me sweet Christ the grace to find --
Son of the Living God!
A small hut in a lonesome spot
To make it my abode.

A little pool but very clear
to stand beside the place
where all men's sins are washed away
by sanctifying grace.

A pleasant woodland all about
to shield it from the wind
and make a home for singing birds
before it and behind.

A southern aspect for the heat --
a stream along its foot.
A smooth green lawn with rich topsoil
propitious to all fruit.

My choice of men to live with me
and pray to God as well --
quiet men of humble mind --
their number I shall tell.

Four files of three, or three of four
to give the Psalter forth;
six to pray by the south church wall
and six along the north.

Two by two my dozen friends --
to tell the number right --
praying with me to move the King
who gives the sun its light.

A lovely church, a home for God
bedecked with linen fine,
where over the white Gospel page
the Gospel candles shine.

A little house where all may dwell
and body's care be sought,
where none shows lust or arrogance,
none thinks an evil thought.

And all I ask for housekeeping --
I get and pay no fees --
leeks from the garden, poultry, game,
salmon and trout and bees.

My share of clothing and of food,
from the King of fairest face,
and I to sit at times alone,
and pray in every place.

9.2 A Celtic Lay Monk Movement

*"A whole new generation of Christians has come up believing that
it is possible to "accept" Christ without forsaking the world."*
*"Prayer will become effective when we stop using it
as a substitute for obedience."*

-A.W. (Aiden Wilson) Tozer (1897-1963)
Evangelist, Pastor, Theologian
Christian & Missionary Alliance
Author: *The Knowledge of the Holy*

———

*"I was no longer the center of my life
and therefore I could see God in everything."*

-The Venerable Bede
Monk, Historian (672/673-735 A.D.)
Author: *The Ecclesiastical History
of the English People*

1999: Founding A *Prayer Encouragement* Ministry

We desired to live more like the ancient Irish Celtic monks who
had so inspired us. Not live like them physically; in a stone beehive-
shaped hermit's hut overlooking the ocean, but spiritually: living holy
lives of purity as *missionary monks* saturated in God's Word:

Reading it, hearing it, memorizing it, living it.

We wanted to pray morning, noon, and night; and even in the middle
of the night! Yes, there was no doubt about it; we wanted to become
monks! There were a few obstacles, of course. Linda was a woman.
Together, we were a married couple.

But mostly, we weren't Roman Catholic or Eastern Orthodox: we
were Evangelical Protestants, and the year was 1999. The biggest
obstacle seemed to be that on the entire Internet *there was no such thing
as a 100% Evangelical Christian monastery, and there had never been
one.*

S.G. Preston

Born Again Protestant Monks

Note: Only 247 million people worldwide were using the Internet in 1999 (by October of 2020, it had reached 4.66 billion users, 59% of Earth's total population of 7.8 billion people). For several months I kept entering into Internet Search Engines the words:

Born Again Protestant Monks.

And not a single organization ever came up. Until we started our own website and put those words at the top of our own Home Page!

Reforming Monasticism: What We Mean By the Term Lay Monks

We wondered…what if Martin Luther had *reformed* the monasteries like he did the Church, instead of just ending them? He had debated whether or not to retain them as schools.

We decided to take up where Luther had left off. Monks have historically been a symbol of a life of consecration to God and dedication to prayer.

To us what was essential to being a *"Lay Monk"* was our statement at the beginning of the first book of this Series, *Prayer as a Total Lifestyle*: *Learning from the Greatest Lives of Prayer*.

What is a *Lay Monk*?

> *"All we really mean by being a 'Lay Monk'*
> *is to be a consecrated Christian,*
> *especially devoted to prayer*
> *and to God's Word."*

(Based on Acts 6:4)

What is an *Evangelical Celtic Lay Monk*?

In *Eastern Orthodox* terminology:

> *We are ordinary Lay Christians emulating Monastics*
> *(as all good Orthodox Christians are encouraged to do).*

———

In *Roman Catholic* terminology:

> *We are Oblates: Third Order Protestant Franciscans.*

———

In *Evangelical Protestant* terminology:

> *We have Reformed Monasticism.*
>
> *(We have applied*
> *Reformation principles to Monasticism,*
> *creating an Evangelical Lay Monasticism*
> *for ordinary Christians;*
> *who may be married or single,*
> *with or without children;*
> *who remain in their own jobs or careers,*
> *and in their own homes and Churches).*

1999 - Married Monks

First of all, we would allow Lay Monks to be married, just like Protestant ministers and priests were after the Reformation. As Orthodox priests have always been allowed to be.

I remember how surprised I was when as a young man I first learned that many Anglican and Eastern Orthodox Priests were married and had children!

Years later, we would learn that some of the ancient Celtic monastic Orders had allowed married monks. It is a matter of historical record that in many cases Abbots would be succeeded in office by their sons.

Note: see *Isle of the Saints: Monastic Settlement and Christian Community in Early Ireland* by Lisa M. Bitel (P. 116)

We would also come to learn that, as far back as the twelfth century, St. Francis of Assisi had conceived the idea of a *Third Order* of Franciscans. We didn't learn this until a few years after we had created our own, very similar, Order! (But it was the first for Protestants.)

The *First Order* of *Friars Minor* was founded for full-time unmarried males. The *Second Order*, The *Sisters of Poor Clare,* was created for full-time unmarried female Franciscans.

S.G. Preston

St. Francis' Third Order

A *Third Order* was also begun for Lay persons, single or married, male or female. It was created by St. Francis specifically for those who desired to be affiliated with a religious Order, while remaining at home in regular jobs and careers, with or without children. Over the centuries, others of the Catholic religious orders have gradually adopted this practice, and such affiliated Lay members are usually referred to as *Oblates*.

Note: St. Francis was the first person to write poetry in Italian, rather than in Latin, which had always been done up until then. He also created the idea of a "Nativity Scene." For the very first Nativity Scene, he used real animals and people, including a real mother and baby.

Full Monk Status for Women

We would also give women Full Monk Status:

> *"...there is neither male nor female;*
> *for you are all one in Christ Jesus."*

> -Galatians 3:28

In 1999 we posted on our website that Monk Linda was *The First Lady Monk*. We did not mean she was the first female monastic! Nuns are female monastics, and they have existed from the beginning of Christian monasticism. Pachomius founded the first women's Convent (Monastery) with his sister, *Amma* Maria, between 318-323 A.D.

The Desert Mothers

I have quoted several of the Desert Fathers (*Abbas*), and one Desert Mother (*Amma*, meaning: *spiritual mother*). I quoted Amma Syncletica earlier (in Section 3.8). I will quote her again at the beginning of the very next Section. There were many more Ammas than just Maria and Syncletica. *The Apothegmata* (*Sayings of the Desert Fathers*) contains forty-seven sayings of the *Desert Mothers*.

Other *Ammas* include St. Paula and her daughter, who aided St. Jerome in monasteries in the Holy Land.

1999 - Monk Linda, *The First Lady Monk*

The Lausiac History, written by Palladius around 419-420 A.D. about the Desert Fathers, counted 2,975 women living as monastics in the Egyptian Desert.

In one of Kathleen Norris' books, *Dakota: A Spiritual Geography* (2001), a group of Catholic Nuns are visiting a Benedictine monastery in North Dakota. They are talking about how they hope someday the Catholic Church will allow female monks. They say they believe it will take at least fifty years. I remember thinking when I read it:

> *"They're dreaming:*
> *the Catholic Church doesn't move that fast."*

It has already happened! Only nineteen years after Monk Linda became *The First Lady Monk* in Christianity, and the first ever on the Internet, there are now today, in 2018, many groups with women Monks, and even at least *one* in the Catholic Church: Fr. Michael Talbot's *Little Portion* Franciscan monastic community.

In any case, Monk Linda became *the first Evangelical born again Christian Lady Monk,* and *the first of the many female Monks* in our own *Knights of Prayer Lay Monastic Order.*™

An Evangelical Lay Monasticism

This new *Evangelical Lay Monasticism* has now become an entire movement. There is currently a growing interest in historic monastic practice across the board throughout most, if not all, Protestant Churches and Denominations.

The Holy Spirit is drawing Christians into deeper communion with Christ through prayer.

Does He not do the same in every generation, because it is so needed in every generation?

9.3 Our Statement of Faith

"Amma Syncletica taught:

*'As that which is poisonous
to the body is removed
by the bitterest of medicines;*

*in the same way,
prayer accompanied
by fasting drives away
evil thoughts.'"*

-Sayings of the Desert Mothers

———

*"Prayer needs fasting
for its full and perfect development.*

*Prayer is the one hand
with which we
grasp the invisible;*

*fasting the other;
with which we let loose
and cast away the visible."*

-Andrew Murray (1828-1917)
Dutch Reformed Pastor
Author: *With Christ in
the School of Prayer*

What We Believe

I composed our Statement of Faith in 1999, at the very beginning of our *PrayerFoundation* ™ ministry.

In doing so, I was greatly indebted to the teaching of two wonderful men of God, and their excellent books:

Fritz Ridenour's *So What's the Difference?*
and Walter Martin's *Kingdom of the Cults.*

Our Statement of Faith

(1.) The Bible is the Word of God, Inerrant in the original autographs.

(2.) There is only One God, Creator of all creation; three Persons in Trinity: Father, Son, and Holy Spirit.

(3.) God became flesh in Christ Jesus; born of a Virgin, conceived of the Holy Spirit.

(4.) Christ atoned for our sins through His death and shed blood on the cross.

(5.) Christ rose bodily from the grave and ascended into Heaven; conquering death and proving that He is God.

(6.) Salvation is only through Christ; available now to all through repentance, faith towards God, and being born again as a new creation in Christ.

(7.) Christ shall return, there will be a final judgment of eternal reward and eternal punishment.

———

Paul's "Romans Road"

I added the *"Romans Road"* of Scripture to our *How to Receive Christ / Romans Road* webpage, after learning there are many versions. In regard to *Romans*: *"It's all good!"* Martin Luther thought all Christians should memorize the entire Book!

My version selects from the generally accepted Scriptures, but keeps them in the order found in the Bible, and limiting them to seven, the Biblical number of *"completeness."*

Romans Road of Scripture

I. Romans 3:10

"As it is written, there are none righteous, no, not one."

II. Romans 3:23

"For all have sinned, and fallen short of the glory of God."

III. Romans 5:8

*"But God has shown his love to us, in that,
while we were yet sinners, Christ died for us."*

IV. Romans 5:12

*"By one man sin entered into the world, and death through sin;
and so death fell upon all men, because all have sinned."*

V. Romans 6:23

*"For the wages of sin is death; but the gift of God is eternal life
through Jesus Christ our Lord."*

VI. Romans 10:9-10

*"That if you shall confess with your mouth the Lord Jesus,
and shall believe in your heart that God has raised Him
from the dead, you shall be saved.*

*For with the heart one believes unto righteousness;
and with the mouth confession is made unto salvation."*

VII. Romans 10:13

*"For whosoever shall call upon the name
of the Lord shall be saved."*

* * *

9.4 The Christian Life is a Life of *Prayer*

*"God's looking for people through whom He can do the impossible;
what a pity we plan only things we can do ourselves."*

*"(In our fast-paced life) we have no time for contemplation.
We have no time to answer God when He calls."*

-A.W. Tozer (1897-1963)
Evangelist, Pastor, Theologian
Christian & Missionary Alliance
Author: *The Knowledge of the Holy*

God's Will for Your Life

We have become Christians. We have had a conversion experience
and received Christ. We have been born again as a new creation of God
through the power of the Holy Spirit. Now what? What do we do next?
God will show you. He will let you know:

Spend time in His Word. Spend time with God in prayer.

Charles Spurgeon taught:

*"All hell is vanquished when the believer
bows his knee in importunate supplication.*

Beloved brethren, let us pray.

*We cannot all argue, but we can all pray.
We cannot all be leaders, but we can all be pleaders.
We cannot all be mighty in rhetoric,
but we can all be prevalent in prayer.*

I would sooner see you eloquent with God than with men.

*Prayer links us with the eternal,
the Omnipotent, the Infinite,
and hence it is our chief resort...*

*Be sure that you are with God,
and then you may be sure
that God is with you."*

As We Have Seen, in the Ultimate and Final Sense, the Scriptures are Both Our *Creed* for *Faith* and Our *Rule* for *Practice*

Is having a formal Creed necessary? No, but it can certainly be helpful. That is why our Ministry has a *Statement of Faith*. It can also be helpful. Every Christian already *has a Creed* (their understanding of Scripture), whether it is a formal one, or not. As Dr. J. Vernon McGee has said: *"'No Creed but the Bible.' and 'No Creed but Christ.'* are two very good Creeds!"

What about monastic *Rules*? Are *they* necessary? I think the answer again is "No." But they too, have been found to be helpful. Monastic Orders have had *Rules* going back through Benedict, Augustine and Basil, all the way to Pachomius. Like the idea of having a *Creed*, as we discovered earlier; the idea of having a *Rule*, you may be surprised to learn, is *also* an Apostolic one, and again is found in the Scriptures themselves:

The Rule of the Apostle Paul

> *"For in Christ Jesus neither circumcision avails anything,*
> *nor uncircumcision, but a new creation.*
>
> *And as many as walk according to this Rule,*
> *peace be upon them, and mercy; and upon the Israel of God."*

-Galatians 6:15-16

The Celtic Cross Rule

Seven sections of Scripture contain the essence of the *Rule* of our Order, which I have called *The Celtic Cross Rule*:

> *"Draw near to God, and He will draw near to you."*

-James 4:8

———

> *"But we will devote ourselves continually to prayer,*
> *and to the ministry of the word."*

-Acts 6:4

———

"For this cause we also,
since the day we heard it,
do not cease to pray for you,

and to desire that you might be filled
with the knowledge of His will
in all wisdom
and spiritual understanding;

that you might walk worthy of the Lord
unto all pleasing,
being fruitful in every good work,
and increasing in the knowledge of God."

-Colossians 1:9-10

——

"Rejoice always.
Pray without ceasing.
In everything give thanks.

For this is the will of God
in Christ Jesus concerning you."

-1 Thessalonians 5:16-18

——

"Evening, and morning, and at noon:
I will pray, and call out loud,
and He shall hear my voice."

-Psalm 55:17

——

"Lord, what would you have me do?

-Acts 9:6

——

"The Lord is near to all that call upon Him;
to all that call upon Him in truth."

-Psalm 145:18

Live like Elijah

To become a man or woman of prayer is to live the Christian life as God intended.

God had 7,000 who did not bow the knee to Baal. They were God's well-beloved children, but they were invisible, secret, and silent. Like Elijah, if the word of God had not told us about them, we would be totally unaware of their existence.

God could use Elijah to fulfill His purpose. Elijah was *one solitary life* who could be used by God *to change the world.* Let us make it our goal to also be that *one* who can be used by God.

You may say that Elijah was *not like* ordinary believers. Who can be like Elijah? The answer is given us in Scripture, which states that Elijah was:

"...subject to the same passions as we are."

But Elijah *was* different in one all-important way. Elijah was *a man of prayer.* Elijah was an ordinary man who could be used by God to *change the history of the world, because* he was a man of prayer. Let us become such men and women of prayer.

Pray like Elijah

"The effective,
fervent prayer of a godly person
accomplishes much.

Elijah was a man subject to the same passions as we are,
and he prayed intensely that it might not rain;
and it did not rain on the earth
for three years and six months.

Then he prayed again,
and the heavens poured down rain,
and the earth produced its fruit."

-James 5:16-18

9.5 Prayers of St. Patrick & St. Francis

"Christ with me, Christ before me,
Christ behind me, Christ in me..."

-From: *St. Patrick's Breastplate Prayer*

———

"Lord, make me an instrument of Thy peace.
Where there is hatred, let me sow love..."

-A Franciscan Prayer

Prayer After Awaking: *St. Patrick's Breastplate Prayer*

This prayer is also known as the *Lorica* and the *Deer's Cry*. It was the *Awaking Prayer* of Irish Celtic Christian Monks for 740 years:

I arise today
through a mighty strength,
the invocation of the Trinity.
Through belief in the Threeness,
through confession of the Oneness
of the Creator of creation.

I arise today
Through the strength of Christ's birth with His baptism,
through the strength of His crucifixion with His burial,
through the strength of His resurrection with His ascension,
through the strength of His descent on the Day of Judgement.

I arise today
Through the strength of the love of cherubim,
in the obedience of angels,
in the service of archangels,
in the hope of resurrection to meet with reward.
In the prayers of patriarchs,
in the predictions of prophets,
in the preaching of apostles,
in the faith of confessors,
in the innocence of holy virgins,
in the deeds of righteous men.

S.G. Preston

I arise today

Through the strength of heaven,
the light of the sun,
the radiance of the moon.
The splendor of fire,
the speed of lightning,
the swiftness of wind,
the depth of the sea,
the stability of the earth,
the firmness of rock.

I arise today

through God's strength to pilot me,
God's might to uphold me,
God's wisdom to guide me,
God's eye to look before me,
God's ear to hear me,
God's word to speak for me,
God's hand to guard me,
God's shield to protect me,
God's host to save me:
From snares of demons,
from temptation of vices,
from everyone who shall wish me ill,
afar and near.

I summon today

all these powers between me and those evils,
against every cruel and merciless power
that may oppose my body and soul.
Against incantations of false prophets,
against black laws of pagandom,
against false laws of heretics,
against craft of idolatry,
against spells of witches and smiths and wizards,
against every knowledge that corrupts man's body and soul.
Christ to shield me today
against poison, against burning,
against drowning, against wounding:
so that there may come to me an abundance of reward.

Christ with me,
Christ before me,
Christ behind me,
Christ in me,
Christ beneath me,
Christ above me.
Christ on my right,
Christ on my left,
Christ when I lie down,
Christ when I sit down,
Christ when I arise.
Christ in the heart of everyone who thinks of me,
Christ in the mouth of everyone who speaks of me,
Christ in every eye that sees me,
Christ in every ear that hears me.

I arise today
through a mighty strength,
the invocation of the Trinity.
Through belief in the Threeness,
through confession of the Oneness
of the Creator of creation.

———

"Yes, the sparrow has found
a house, and the swallow
a nest for herself,
where she may
lay her young:
even your altars,
O LORD of Hosts;
my King and my God."

-Psalm 84:3

———

"Ask the animals and they shall teach you;
ask the birds of the air and they shall tell you;
or speak to the earth and it shall teach you,
and the fish of the sea shall declare it to you:

S.G. Preston

Which of all these does not know
that the hand of the Lord has done this?
In whose hand is the soul of every living thing,
and the breath of all mankind."

-Job 12:7-10

St. Francis is the Patron Saint of Animals, and of Ecology. His Feast Day is October 4, when many Churches will pray for your pets. As Celtic Christian Lay Monks in the spirit of St. Francis, we are greatly inspired by his life and example.

We have therefore chosen to memorize and pray this prayer nightly before retiring to sleep. It is engraved on a plaque placed on the wall, where it is the first thing seen when someone enters our Monastery. This prayer was not written by St. Francis, but it sums up his beliefs and teachings very well.

Prayer Before Sleep: *Lord, Make Me an Instrument of Thy Peace*

Lord, make me an instrument of Thy peace.
Where there is hatred, let me sow love;
where there is injury, pardon;
where there is doubt, faith;
where there is despair, hope;
where there is darkness, light;
where there is sadness, joy.

O Divine Master,
grant that I may not so much seek
to be consoled as to console;
to be understood, as to understand;
to be loved, as to love.

For it is in giving that we receive;
it is in pardoning, that we are pardoned;
it is in dying that we are born to eternal life.

* * *

9.6 Prayer: A Sabbath Island in Time

"Mas math leat sith,
cairdeas, agus cluain –
eisd, faic, 'us fuirich samhach."

"If you wish peace,
friendship, and quietness:
listen, look, and be silent."

-Old Gaelic Saying

——

"The LORD is in His holy Temple;
let all the earth keep silence before Him."

-Habakkuk 2:20

——

"To fast is to banquet with Angels."

-Athanasius of Alexandria (c. 293-373 A.D.)
Bishop; Author: *On the Incarnation*

Holy Island

I had come to that place in life where I realized that there was no meaning in anything other than in serving Christ.

I wanted to grow closer to God in prayer. I wanted more of Christ.

Lindisfarne (Holy Island) is completely surrounded by water only when the tide is in. Pilgrims wait for the tide to go out and the narrow land bridge to appear, which they can then walk across to reach the island.

Aidan was thinking of this, when he wrote about the balance the Celtic monks practiced, between contemplative lives of prayer and the active sharing of the Good News of Christ with the world.

I posted *Aidan's Prayer* in the very front of this book, and repeat it here because it sums up what it means for me to live as a Celtic Lay Monk.

S.G. Preston

Aidan's Prayer

"Leave me alone with God as much as may be.

As the tide draws the waters
close in upon the shore,
make me an island, set apart,
alone with You, God,
holy to You.

Then, with the turning of the tide,
prepare me to carry Your presence
to the busy world beyond,
the world that rushes
in on me,

until the waters return
and enfold me back to you."

Solitude: Be Still, and Know That I Am God (Psalm 46:10)

Today, this day that the Lord has made, began with me seated cross-legged outdoors on our monastery's deck at sunrise, where I have decided to devote all day on a water fast, mostly to prayer, but also to reading the Bible; while maintaining a still and quiet awareness and appreciation of God and His creation.

When we fast, we are detached from this world; we walk about feeling as though we are Angels, finally living only on:

"...every word that proceeds
out of the mouth
of God."

-Matthew 4:4

The hours pass, crawling lazily by at the pace of a snail. A sleepy snail. Hermiston eats a little, drinks some water; barks, chases, naps.

When he wakes up, he eats a little, drinks some water; barks, chases, naps.

Such a Day is One of the Best

All day long. Hermiston seems to be perfectly at one with the day, with God, and with himself.

I am seated exactly at his level, seeing the world from his quite different point of view.

Squirrels dart about in short bursts; clouds barely move, drifting ever so slowly through the summer sky. Chirping birds land only to fly away again.

The sun moves slowly across the sky and spectacularly sets. Such a day is one of the best.

A Foretaste of Heaven

Brother Lawrence, in the monastery kitchen with his pots and pans, spoke of *practicing the presence of God*; of being aware of God every waking moment; as one way of *praying without ceasing*: thinking our every thought to God.

Yet it is also good to set aside a certain time every day to pray without distraction.

An hour of the day, set aside for prayer, is like *a Sabbath island in time*, in which we are temporarily free of all the time pressures and constraints of this life.

For me, this is a good beginning.
I find it to be a foretaste of Heaven.

Nothing is required of us,
and we are free at last
to only worship God.

* * * * *

S.G. Preston

Recommended Ministry

Redeem TV Streaming Goodness. (Our Favorite TV Channel!)

Christian Film Streaming Service founded by Bill Curtis, President of *Vision Video / Christian History Institute*.

> *"A donor-supported, ad-free, streaming service with no fees. Our goal is to provide edifying and redemptive visual media content for all ages."*

redeemtv.com   watch.redeemtv.com

Christian History Magazine (Our Favorite Magazine!)

Published four times per year, and available by donation through the *Christian History Institute* ministry. We have subscribed for over a decade and have collected back issues of all but four of the over 125 past issues. It is always exciting to receive each new issue!

christianhistoryinstitute.org

Recommended Books

In Bold: Must Read (or: **Must Listen To** on Audiobook if available).
In Italics: *Highly Recommended*
Not in Italics: Recommended.

Prayer

"Power Through Prayer" by E.M. Bounds

"The Kneeling Christian" (Anonymous)

"Hudson Taylor's Spiritual Secret" by Dr. Taylor

"George Muller: Delighted in God" by Roger Steer

"The Practice of the Presence of God" by Brother Lawrence

"Prayer" by O. Hallesby

"Psalms: The Prayer Book of the Bible" by Dietrich Bonhoeffer

(All other books on prayer by E.M. Bounds)

"The Path of Celtic Prayer" by Calvin Miller

"The Path of Prayer" by Samuel Chadwick

"The Power of Prayer" by R.A. Torrey

"With Christ in the School of Prayer" by Andrew Murray

"The Life and Diary of David Brainerd" Edited by Jonathan Edwards (Scholarly)

Basic Christian Teaching

"Mere Christianity" by C.S. Lewis

"Knowing God" by J.I. Packer

"Growing in Christ" by J.I. Packer

"God Wrote a Book" by James McDonald

"Spiritual Disciplines for the Christian Life" by Donald S. Whitney

"Christ, Baptism and the Lord's Supper: Recovering the Sacraments for Evangelicals" by Leonard Vander Zee

"The Confessions" by St. Augustine

"On the Incarnation" by St. Athanasius of Alexandria (Scholarly)

"The Didache: The Teaching of the Twelve Apostles" (Church Manual: Late 1st to Early 2nd Century)

"The Knowledge of the Holy" by A.W. Tozer

"Basic Christianity" by John R.W. Stott

Christian Life

"L'Abri" by Edith Schaeffer (Autobiography)

"Desiring God" by John Piper (Teaching)

"E.M. Bounds: Man of Prayer" by Lyle Dorsett (Biography)

"St. Francis of Assisi" by Omer Englebert (Biography)

Daily Devotional:

"The Imitation of Christ" by Thomas à Kempis

Celtic Christianity / Celtic Monasticism

"How the Irish Saved Civilization" by Thomas Cahill (second half of book only, from *St. Patrick* on: History of Irish Celtic Monasticism)

(Note: This is a book written by a Secular Author)

"Sun Dancing" by Geoffrey Moorhouse (History of Monks at *Skellig Michael*)

(Note: This is a book written by a Secular Author)

"Celtic Christianity: Yesterday, Today, and for the Future" by Paul D.J. Arblaster

"Flame in My Heart: St Aidan for Today" by David Adam

"The Path of Celtic Prayer" by Calvin Miller

"Thin Places: An Evangelical Journey into Celtic Christianity" by Tracy Balzer

"The Celtic Way of Evangelism" by George G. Hunter III

Early Church Teaching and Practice

"Reading Scripture with the Church Fathers" by Christopher A. Hall

"Learning Theology with the Church Fathers" by Christopher A. Hall

"Worshipping with the Church Fathers" by Christopher A. Hall

"Living Wisely with the Church Fathers" by Christopher A. Hall

"Ancient-Future Faith" by Robert E. Webber

"Ancient-Future Worship" by Robert E. Webber

"Ancient-Future Time" by Robert E. Webber

"The Sign of the Cross: The Gesture, the Mystery, the History" by Andreas Andreopoulos

"Getting to Know the Church Fathers: An Evangelical Introduction" by Bryan Litfin

"Beyond Smells and Bells: The Wonder and Power of Christian Liturgy" by Mark Galli

"A New Song for an Old World: Musical Thought in the Early Church" by Calvin R. Stapert

"Evangelicals and Nicene Faith: Reclaiming the Apostolic Witness" Editor, Timothy George

"Retrieving the Tradition & Renewing Evangelicalism: A Primer for Suspicious Protestants" by D.H. Williams (Perhaps *too basic* for most Celtic Lay Monks – perfect to give to the skeptical!)

Christian History

"Here I Stand: A Life of Martin Luther" by Roland Bainton

"Church History in Plain Language" by Bruce L. Shelley

"History of the Christian Church," Volumes 1-6 by Philip Schaff

"The Ecclesiastical History of the English People" by the Venerable Bede (Only the section on the ancient Celtic Monks; Scholarly)

"The History of the Church: From Christ to Constantine" by Eusebius (Scholarly)

Note: The books directly below are some of my all-time favorite books. I've read them three times each (so far) but I realize that they are not for everyone. *If* you are a Christian who *loves the History of Christian Doctrine and Liturgy* they are **must read**:

"Credo" by Jaroslav Pelikan (Scholarly)

"The Christian Tradition," Volumes 1-5, by Jaroslav Pelikan (Scholarly)

"The Shape of the Liturgy" by Dom Gregory Dix (Scholarly)

S.G. Preston

Apologetics

"I Don't Have Enough Faith to Be an Atheist" by Norman L. Geisler and Frank Turek

Excellent Audio Bibles

Word of Promise (**Dramatic Audio Theater:** *New King James Version*) Old and New Testament (Available separately or together). Read by Innumerable Top Actors and Actresses – listens like a Movie Soundtrack. Thomas Nelson Publishers. Our favorite!

New Testament Read by Johnny Cash (*New King James Version*).

Holy Bible NIV Read by David Suchet (Complete Bible: New International Version) (Suchet played: *Hercule Poirot*" in the Television Series).

Excellent Audio Bible Commentary

Thru the Bible Radio: **Dr. J. Vernon McGee** (Commentary on the Entire Bible) 5-Year Radio Program: listen daily on Christian AM Radio. Available on CD at ttb.org or on MP3 elsewhere. I've listened to the entire Commentary at least 6 times and look forward to listening to Dr. McGee off and on for life! Also available in Book form, which we also have (the transcribed Radio talks), for reference use. (**www.ttb.org**)

Note: Our original Website: **www.prayerfoundation.org** Reviews over 200 Christian Books.

Recommended Films

(In Bold) Must See
(*In Italics*) *Highly Recommended*

Full-Length Films:

"Brother Sun, Sister Moon" by Franco Zefirelli (early ministry of St. Francis)

"Luther" (Joseph Fiennes)

"The Nativity Story" (Keisha Castle-Hughes)

"Esther" (Bible Collection: F. Murray Abraham, Louise Lombard) (Made for TV: 1 Hr.)

"St. Patrick: The Irish Legend" (Patrick Bergin, Malcolm McDowell). Excellent! But some may not like that fictional "Legendary" stories are also included.

"Hudson Taylor"

"God's Outlaw: William Tyndale"

"John Wycliffe, The Morning Star"

"John Wesley" (J. Arthur Rank)

"The Gospel of John" (Word for Word: *Good News Bible*) The Film is fantastic! (The additional Commentary at the end is worthless: we recommend not watching it).

Mini-Series

"Jesus of Nazareth" by Franco Zefirelli

Docudramas

"Martin Luther" (PBS)

"St. Patrick: Apostle of Ireland" (includes the complete actual words of St. Patrick)

"Patrick" (narrated by Liam Neeson)

"Robber of the Cruel Streets" (About: George Muller)

"Aidan" (Memorable Leaders in Christian History)

"Oswald" (Memorable Leaders in Christian History)

"Lindisfarne Gospels" (Memorable Leaders in Christian History)

S.G. Preston

Documentaries

"A History of Christian Worship: Ancient Ways, Future Paths" (6 DVDs)
"History of Christianity" (6 Parts on 2 DVDs) by Dr. Timothy George
"Obstacle to Comfort: The Life of George Muller"

Celtic Christian

"And God Came to Ireland" by Hilary Patrick

"My Journey to Life: On the Trail of Celtic Saints" by Rainer Walde

"Blessing Europe: The Legacy of the Celtic Saints" by Rainer Walde

Note: Our Website, **www.prayerfoundation.org** Reviews over 200 Christian Films. *VisionVideo.com* carries these and thousands of other excellent Christian Films.

Bibliography

Primary Sources

Adomnan of Iona, St.; *Life of St. Columba* (Penguin Books, 1995)

à Kempis, Thomas; *The Imitation of Christ* (Random House, 1998)

Athanasius, St.; *On the Incarnation*; (St. Vladimir's Seminary Press, 2003)

Athanasius, St.; *Life of Antony* (Ancient Christian Writer's Series; Paulist Press 1950)

Augustine, St.; *The City of God* (Hendrickson Publishing, 2009)

Augustine, St.; *The Confessions* (Barnes & Noble, 2007)

Benedict, St.; *The Rule of St. Benedict* (Random House, 1998)

Bede, St.; The Venerable; *The Ecclesiastical History of the English People* (Translated by Leo Sherley-Price; Penguin Books, 1990)

Bede, St., The Venerable; *The Life and Miracles of St. Cuthbert, Bishop of Lindisfarne* (Internet History Sourcebook Project; Fordham University)

Basil the Great, St.; *The Hexameron* (CreateSpace Publishing, 2014)

Basil the Great, St.; *Monastic Rule of St. Basil the Great* (Athletis Publishing, 2018)

Bonhoeffer, Dietrich; *The Cost of Discipleship* (Touchstone, 1995)

Bonhoeffer, Dietrich; *Psalms: The Prayer Book of the Bible* (Augsburg, 1970)

Bounds, E.M.; *Power Through Prayer* (Destiny Image, 2007)

Bounds, E.M.; *The Complete Works of E.M. Bounds On Prayer* (Baker Books, 1990)

Brainerd, David; *The Life and Diary of David Brainerd*; Edited by Jonathan Edwards (Baker Books, 1989)

Brother Lawrence; *The Practice of the Presence of God* (Baker Books, 1989)

Cassian, John; *The Conferences* (Translated by Boniface Ramsay, O.P.; Newman Press, 1997)

Cassian, John; *The Institutes* (Translated by Boniface Ramsay, O.P.; Newman Press, 2000)

Catholic Encyclopedia, The; Pope Honorius I, Entry by J. Chapman; New York: Robert Appleton Company, 1910)

Climacus, John; *The Ladder of Divine Ascent* (Paulist Press, 1982)

S.G. Preston

David, Patti; *New Treatment for Brain Problem Available* (*KBOO Guide*; Jan. 1998)

Davies, Oliver; Translator, *Celtic Spirituality* (Paulist Press, 1999)

Didache, or The Teaching of the Twelve Apostles (Translated by James A. Kleist, S.J., Ph.D.; Newman Press, 1948)

Eusebius; *The History of the Church: From Christ to Constantine* (Penguin Books, 1989)

Foxe, John; *Foxe's Book of Martyrs* (Bridge-Logos, 2001)

Harmless, William S.J.; Apothegmata Patrum: Text and Context (Sayings of the Desert Fathers; Oxford Scholarship Online; 2005)

Harrison, Becky; *CD: "Take It Easy"* (*KBOO Guide*; Jan. 1998)

Hippolytus; *On the Apostolic Tradition* (St. Vladimir's Seminary Press, 2001)

Irenaeus of Lyon, St.; *Against Heresies,* Books 1-3 (Paulist Press, 2012)

Josephus, Flavius; *The Life* (CreateSpace, 2013)

Lewis, C.S.; *Mere Christianity* (HarperCollins, 1996)

Lewis, C.S.; *Letters to Malcolm: Chiefly On Prayer* (HarperCollins, 1984)

Luther, Martin; *Luther's Small Catechism* (Concordia, 2017)

Murray, Andrew; *With Christ in the School of Prayer* (Classic Reprint, 2017)

Norris, Kathleen; *Dakota: A Spiritual Geography* (Mariner Books, 2001)

O'Maiden, Uinsean, OCR (Translator, *The Celtic Monk: Rules and Writings of Early Irish Monks* (Cistercian Publications, 1996)

Oxford English Dictionary (Oxford University Press, 2012)

Packer, J.I.; *Growing In Christ* (Crossway Books, 2007)

Packer, J.I.; *Knowing God* (InterVarsity Press, 1973)

Palladius, *The Lausiac History* (Ancient Christian Writers Series, No. 34; Paulist Press, 1965)

Patrick of Ireland, St.; *The Works of St. Patrick* (Ancient Christian Writers Series, No. 17; Paulist Press, 1953)

Service Books of the Orthodox Church (St. Tikhon's Monastic Press, 2013):
    The Divine Liturgy of St. Basil the Great
    The Divine Liturgy of St. John Chrysostom

Spurgeon, Charles; *Spiritual Warfare In A Believer's Life* (YWAM Publishing, 1996)

Spurgeon, Charles; *The Treasury of David*; (Commentary on the Psalms; Updated Edition in Today's Language; Thomas Nelson, 1997)

Tertullian, *On Prayer* (Kessinger Publishing, 2015)

Tertullian, *The Chaplet, or De Corona* (Lighthouse Publishing, 2015)

Tertullian, Quintas Septimus; *The Shows or De Spectaculis* (CreateSpace, 2015)

Theodoretus, Bishop of Cyrus; *Eccclesiastical History* (Classic Reprint, 2012)

Thoreau, Henry David; *Walden: Or, Life in the Woods* (Houghton Mifflin, 2004)

Tolkien, J.R.R.; *Tree and Leaf* (HarperCollins, 2001)

Torrey, R. A.; *The Power of Prayer* (Zondervan, 1971)

Tozer, A.W.; *The Knowledge of the Holy* (HarperCollins, 1961)

Vincent of Lérins; *The Commonitory of St. Vincent of Lérins*; Paul A. Boer Sr. Editor (Veritatis Splendor Publications, 2012)

Secondary Sources

Adam, David; *Fire of the North: The Illustrated life of St. Cuthbert* (SPCK, 1993)

Adam, David; *Flame in My Heart: St. Aidan for Today* (Morehouse Publishing, 1998)

Andreopoulos, Andreas; *The Sign of the Cross: The Gesture, the Mystery, the History* (Paraclete Press, 2006)

Arblaster, Paul D.J.; *Celtic Christianity: Yesterday, Today, and for the Future* (Virtualbookworm.com, 2002)

Bitel, Lisa M.; *Isle of the Saints: Monastic Settlement and Christian Community in Early Ireland* (Cornell University Press, 1990)

Bainton, Roland; *Here I Stand; A Life of Martin Luther* (Penguin Books, 1995)

Cahill, Thomas; *How the Irish Saved Civilization* (Doubleday, 1995)

Dix, Dom Gregory; *The Shape of the Liturgy* (Continuum, 1945)

Dorsett, Lyle W.; *E.M. Bounds: Man of Prayer* (Zondervan, 1991)

Encyclopaedia Britannica (1911), Vol. 14, Page 789 (Ireland, Church of)

S.G. Preston

Englebert, Omer; *St. Francis of Assisi: A Biography*; Transl. by Eve Marie Cooper (Servant Books, 1979)

Hunter III, George G.; *The Celtic Way of Evangelism: How Christianity Can Reach the West...Again* (Abingdon Press, 2000)

International Standard Bible Encyclopedia, 1915; Orr, James, M.A., D.D., General Editor (Entry for: "Hours of Prayer" by Henry E. Dosker)

Moorhouse, Geoffrey; *Sun Dancing* (Harcourt Brace & Company, 1997)

Oden, Thomas; General Editor; *Ancient Christian Doctrine,* Vol. 1-5 (IVP Academic, 2009)

Oden, Thomas, Gen. Ed.; *Ancient Christian Commentary On Scripture,* 29 Volumes (InterVarsity Press, 2005)

Papavassiliou, Vassilios; (Commentary on) Climacus, St. John; *Thirty Steps to Heaven: The Ladder of Divine Ascent for All Walks of Life* (Ancient Faith Publishing, 2014)

Pelikan, Jaroslav; *The Christian Tradition,* Vol. 1-5 (University of Chicago Press, 1971)

Pelikan, Jaroslav; *Credo* (Yale University Press, 2003)

Philokalia, The; Vol. 1-4 (Faber and Faber, 1983)

Schaff, Philip; *History of the Christian Church,* Vol. 1-8 (Hendrickson, 2006)

Schatz, Klaus, S.J.; *Papal Primacy: From its Origins to the Present* (Liturgical Press; Collegeville, Minnesota; 1996).

Index

Note: There are no entries for certain words: including *Christ*, *Holy Spirit*, *Christianity*, and *Prayer*; because they are mentioned or implied on nearly every page.

A

S.G. Preston

Anglican; 60, 93, 132, 142, 145, 146, 171, 175, 204, 228
Anglican Mission in the Americas; 204
Annaghdown, Ireland (Brendan's Death); 66
Answers to Prayer; 52, 60, 68, 130, 143
Answers to Prayer (Book); iv, 28, 52, 68, 90, 109, 110, 164, 193, 222
    Excerpts from:
        France: Ban Lifted on *Passion of the Christ* Film; 28
        India: Hostages Released; 52
        Israel: Woman Recovered from Mastectomy, Lupus, and Chemotherapy; 68
        Italy: Daughter Delivered from Depression; 90
        Russia: Evangelical Seminary Passes Inspection; 109, 110
        Afghanistan: Christian Aid Workers Freed From Taliban; 130
        Samoa: Ban of Chieftans Ended; 164
        Pennsylvania: Finances, False Charges Dropped, Son Off Heroin; 193
        India: Muslim Father, 90, Accepts Christ; 222
Antichrist; 67
Antioch, Episcopal See of; 41, 42
Appennine Mountains, Northern Italy; 62
Apostles, Apostolic; 42, 69, 75, 123, 127, 166, 167, 168, 170, 176, 178, 179, 181,
    184, 216, 238
Apothegmata (Sayings of the Desert Fathers); 229
Apostle James;127
Apostle John; 127, 180, 186
Apostle Paul; 153, 163, 183, 190, 232, 235
Apostle Peter; 70, 104, 180, 185, 186
Apostle to Ireland (St. Patrick); 59
Arblaster, (Brother) Paul; 194, 195, 196, 197, 198, 199
    Author: *Celtic Christianity Yesterday, Today, and for the Future*; 194, 196, 197
Arblaster, Carol (Harpist, Music CDs); 196, 197, 199
Archangel Michael; 48
Arian Heresy; 61, 81
Arius of Alexandria, Bishop; 61
Aran Islands, Ireland; 64
Arizona, 124
Arkansas; 15
Armageddon; 67
Armagh; 24
Armor of God; 163
Archbishop; 57
Arthur, King; 163, 195
Arran Islands, Scotland (Brendan Visits); 64
Arterial Venus Malformations (AVMs); 201
Arvada, Colorado; 20
Ascension of Christ; 238
A Shepherd Looks at the 23rd Psalm by W. Phillip Keller; 198
A Shepherd Looks at The Lord's Prayer by W. Phillip Keller; 198

S.G. Preston

Bishop of Rome (see: Pope)
Bishop Erc of Slane; (Brendan's Teacher); 63, 64
Bitel, Lisa; Author, *Isle of the Saints: Monastic Settlement and Christian Community in Early Ireland*; 228
Blarney Stone, Blarney Castle, Ireland; 30
Bloxwich, England; 194
Bobbio, Italy (Columbanus' Monastery); 63
Bonhoeffer, Dietrich; 131, 132, 133, 134, 135
    The Cost of Discipleship; 131
    Psalms: The Prayer Book of the Bible; 131, 132, 133, 134, 135
Book of Durrow (Columba): 71
Book of Kells (Columba) 71
Born Again Protestant Monks; 227
Boston, Massachusetts; 31
Bounds, E.M.; 94, 116, 117, 144, 179
Bourbon Street; 125
Brainerd, David; 111
Brain Problem; 200
Brandon's Mountain (Brendan's); 34
Brazil; 94
Breastplate Prayer of St. Patrick; Title Page, 238, 239, 240
Brendan the Navigator, St.; 34, 62, 64
Brigid of Kildare, St. (or: Brigit, or: Bridget); 44, 63
Britain; 36, 53, 54, 55, 56, 57, 58, 59, 151
British Columbia, Canada; 97
British Empire; 155
British Parliament; 155
Brits; 205
Brittany, France (Brendan Visits); 64
Brother Andrew; 14, 207
    Author: *God's Smuggler*; 207
Brother Danny; 199
    (see: Lay Monk Danny)
Brother Lawrence; 88, 244
Brother Paul; 194, 198
Brude, King of Northern Picts (Scotland, Columba); 76
Bullinger, Heinrich; *Second Helvetic Confession* (1566); 172, 174, 175
    Zwingli, Ulrich; 172
Bunratty Castle, Ireland; 30
Bunyan, John; 105
Byzantium; 47, 61
    (See: Eastern Orthodox)

C

D

F

G

H

I

J

K

L

S.G. Preston

Author: *With Christ in the School of Prayer*; 103, 231
Music CDs; 195, 199, 200, 202
Music Guide Magazine; 200

N

O

P

Q

R

U

V

W

S.G. Preston

X

X-Games Skiers and U.S. Olympic Team; 100
   Mt. Hood, Oregon (Skiing on Palmer Glacier); 100

Y

Yang, Fenggang; Purdue University's Center on Religion and Chinese Society; 207
YMCA; 121
Your Comments; 11, 12, 13, 14, 15, 16, 17, 18, 19, 20, 21, 22, 23, 196
Youth Pastor; 205
Youth Leader; 205
Youth With a Mission (YWAM); 11, 14, 207

Z

Zinzendorf, Count; 207
Zwingli, Ulrich; 172
   Second Helvetic Confession by Heinrich Bullinger; 172

Pax Et Bonum!
May God richly bless you as you serve Him!
Yours in Christ,
-Lay Monk Preston & Lay Monk Linda